MINNESOTA
OPEN HOUSE

Purcell-Cutts House, Minneapolis

MINNESOTA OPEN HOUSE

A Guide to Historic House Museums

Krista Finstad Hanson

Minnesota Historical Society Press

www.mhspress.org

The Minnesota Historical Society Press is a member of the
Association of American University Presses.

Manufactured in Canada

10 9 8 7 6 5 4 3 2 1

∞ The paper used in this publication meets the minimum
requirements of the American National Standard for
Information Sciences—Permanence for Printed Library
Materials, ANSI Z39.48-1984.

Credits
Front cover: Glensheen, Duluth, by Bob King, Duluth
Back cover: Fictional home of Maud Hart Lovelace's "Tacy,"
    Mankato, courtesy Betsy-Tacy Society, Mankato, and Schiroo
    Cabin, Hutchinson, courtesy McLeod County Historical Society
Interior: Unless otherwise noted, photos by Krista Finstad
    Hanson and Paul E. Hanson
Maps: Paul E. Hanson, St. Paul
Design: Percolator, Minneapolis

International Standard Book Number
ISBN 13: 978-0-87351-577-1 (paper)
ISBN 10: 0-87351-577-3 (paper)

Library of Congress Cataloging-in-Publication Data

Hanson, Krista Finstad.
    Minnesota open house : a guide to historic house museums /
    Krista Finstad Hanson.
        p. cm.
    ISBN-13: 978-0-87351-577-1 (paper : alk. paper)
    ISBN-10: 0-87351-577-3 (paper : alk. paper)
        1. Historic buildings—Minnesota—Guidebooks.
        2. Dwellings—Minnesota—Guidebooks.
        3. Historic sites—Minnesota—Guidebooks.
        4. Historical museums—Minnesota—Guidebooks.
        5. Minnesota—Guidebooks.
        6. Minnesota—History, Local.
        I. Title.
F607.H26 2007
917.760454—dc22

                                                    2006028795

ACKNOWLEDGMENTS

This book began as an idea about a decade ago. Although I wrote a Wisconsin version of this survey of historic house museums first, a Minnesota book was never far from my mind. I have been touring the state's museums since 2001, but I made a concerted effort to visit sites over the summers of 2004 and 2005.

Traveling around this large and lovely state, I have been accompanied on occasion by my husband, Paul Hanson, and my children, Eva and Wyatt. Most of the time, however, I have visited the museums on my own, a very real pleasure for a busy mother. I am grateful to five babysitters over the years, to my mother Marie and stepfather Singh Grewal, to my sister Anje Schmitz, and of course to my husband, all of whom have cared for the children while I traveled.

Information in this book comes directly from my tours of the museums and from printed and web-based information provided by the museums, as well as from numerous e-mails and phone queries fielded by museum staff members and site directors. To them I am most grateful. This book would not have been possible without their assistance.

Many Minnesota Historical Society staff members were immensely helpful to me, including Heather Koop, Tom Ellig, Tim Glines, David Grabitske, and the historic site directors. I am indebted to publisher Greg Britton at the Minnesota Historical Society Press, who has been committed to this project for all these years and who provided essential help. My editor, Marilyn Ziebarth, worked diligently to make this a cogent and cohesive book. Press intern Melissa Johnson helped along the way. My thanks also go to Will Powers for the expert production work and to my husband, Paul, for the helpful maps. Thanks to Anne Levin, dear friend, for her research and indexing assistance.

Thanks to Paul for taking some of the photographs. Most were taken using Kodak Ektachrome 200 transparency (slide) film.

My dear Great Aunt Rie started me on this passionate journey of visiting house museums when I was a young girl growing up in Wisconsin. Each summer she took my siblings, cousins, and me to countless museums in our corner of the world.

My own internal fires are fueled by my love for historical research and writing, but the flames are fanned by my friends in the writing trade and by friends who know the power of pursuing a dream. Thank you for listening to my tales and encouraging me along the way. I am grateful there are so many of you.

Thank you also to my writing mentors within and without the University of Wisconsin–Eau Claire, who first guided me towards nonfiction, helped me along toward early publications, and continue to inspire and support me. Thanks go to John Hildebrand, Bill Nolte, Frank Smoot, and Bruce Taylor.

I am grateful for the community of like-minded souls at the Minnesota chapter of the Society of Architectural Historians. Thank you for being my first audience in 2001.

Finally, I knowingly followed in the footsteps of David Gebhard, Tom Martinson, and Roger Kennedy, whose works on Minnesota architecture I used regularly as references.

CONTENTS

SOUTHEAST REGION 188

INTRODUCTION

I am constantly surprised at the humble beauty and regal elegance found in Minnesota's historic houses. When I tour a small log cabin cozily furnished with handmade items and learn that a family of twelve once lived in this one-loft-no-bath place, I am impressed by the early residents' tenacity and strength. Each time I attend an event at the James J. Hill House or Alexander Ramsey House, I think back to generations of people who would have loved just one peek inside these stately homes far, far beyond their means. Today's diverse house museums allow us to learn about the tremendous scope of Minnesota's history, from the hardships of making do on the frontier to the lavish lifestyles of wealthy businessmen.

The state's residents have long believed it important to preserve historic places. The territorial legislature and

In 1896, Minneapolis children help move the John H. Stevens House in an early community preservation effort. *(Minnesota Historical Society [MHS])*

Governor Alexander Ramsey, whose early-1870s retirement house is preserved in St. Paul, established the Minnesota Historical Society in 1849 to preserve and share Minnesota history for generations to come. Sarah Jane Sibley, whose late-1830s house is preserved in Mendota, organized a statewide preservation effort in 1859 that raised money to restore, preserve, and interpret George Washington's Mount Vernon estate. (Her own home, the oldest remaining private house in Minnesota, would be saved later by the Daughters of the American Revolution and opened to the public as a museum.) It was not until 1896, however, when 7,000 Minneapolis schoolchildren literally helped move the 1850 John H. Stevens House to a new site, that the historic preservation movement was fully launched in Minnesota. While citizens began to advocate preserving Historic Fort Snelling as early as 1863, completion of that task remained for countless local and national preservationists a hundred years later. The fort's 1824 Commanding Officer's Quarters, now open to the public, is the oldest remaining home in Minnesota.

These museums have wonderful stories about how they came to be. Visitors can learn how a committee saved a precious house from being torn down or how foresighted benefactors saved belongings and kept their homes intact with the hope of making them into museums. Some house museums began during the 1976 United States Bicentennial, when many civic groups chose house restorations as their Bicentennial projects. The Minnesota Historical Society, funded in part by taxpayers, has a long history of maintaining historic house museums, as well as helping county historical societies around the state tell the story of our shared history.

While each museum offers a place to learn about Minnesota history and how people lived in times past, many sites offer additional features and programs. Some are home to or affiliated with a county historical society. These societies contain local historical archives used by genealogists and others interested in researching local history. Frequent family-friendly events at many sites include high teas, pig roasts, buffalo feeds, harvest festivals, and Christmas-decoration tours. Special events include lectures, themed tours, and historical reenactments of settler handicrafts and skills.

My goal has been to provide a travel guide showcasing Minnesota's wealth of historic homes, from log cabins to grand mansions, which are open to the public and can be toured as museums. Some of these houses are included in living-history villages. "Houses," as I defined them in this book, also include recreated frontier forts and recreated Native American dwellings. Nearly two hundred such museums are included in this guidebook.

The house museums described are open to the public on a regular basis. Not listed are museums that serve as primary residences or businesses, thus excluding bed-and-breakfast establishments and antique shops housed in old homes that sometimes offer tours.

The text accompanying each museum's description is based on information provided by the museum's staff or websites. Entries provide general historical information and a brief overview of the sights and attractions offered at the museum. Hopefully, the entries will spark interest and encourage readers to visit the sites. Additional museum information comes from the texts listed at the end of this book and related Internet sites. I attempted to reach all museum directors to have them review their entry, and I personally visited most of the museums, taking a full tour of three-quarters of the museums. My husband, Paul, and I took the photos, with the exception of a few provided by the museums themselves.

I hope you enjoy this book and appreciate the volunteers and staff who care for these treasured spaces. These houses have the capacity to transport us into the past and teach us something new about ourselves. Perhaps you will return to the sites and become a historical society member or volunteer. The survival of these museums for future generations depends upon your support!

Happy travels.
Krista Finstad Hanson

NORTHWEST

NORTHEAST

CENTRAL

METRO

SOUTHWEST

SOUTHEAST

N

0 20 40 60 80 Miles

GUIDE TO USING THIS BOOK

Maps The state is divided into six geographical regions: Metropolitan, Central, Northwest, Northeast, Southwest, and Southeast. These delineations are somewhat arbitrary, so a county sometimes associated with the northeast of the state, for example, may be included in the central region.

Directions A brief address has been provided for each site. Because many of these house and cabin museums are definitely off the beaten path, it is highly recommended that visitors call ahead for directions. Internet mapping sites may also be useful. Gas stations, city halls, and town libraries also have helpful people who can offer assistance.

Open Seasons Many of these museums have a limited season of operation. Some may be open as infrequently as the third Sunday afternoon during June, July and August. Many of the museums are open only during the prime summer tourism season, Memorial Day through Labor Day, yet also have a fall event and perhaps a Christmas celebration with house decorations. Other sites are open on a year-around basis. Nearly all of these museums are open by advanced appointment for group tours.

Hours Visitors are urged to phone the museums for their current hours of operation. Some of the phone numbers are for private residences, since many museums are run completely by volunteers. Phone numbers (and area codes) change frequently, so a call to the local chamber of commerce or visitor's bureau may also assist in reaching a museum.

Fees Many of the museums charge small entrance fees. Many museums charge reduced rates for groups, seniors, and children. Minnesota Historical Society membership, like membership in many local historical societies and associations, carries free admission to its sites. All the museums welcome your donations.

More information Many of these museums have websites of their own. While some websites are updated regularly, some are not. The Minnesota Department of Tourism's website is kept up to date, and many of these museums are featured on that website. In addition, the Minnesota Historical Society website posts current information for its own museums and has a county historical society link on the homepage.

NOTE: Sites listed on the National Register of Historic Places are marked with the following symbol: �

Minnesota Historical Society historic sites are marked with the following symbol: ᴍ

MINNESOTA
OPEN HOUSE

William E. Goodfellow Mansion, Minneapolis

METRO REGION

1   Anoka County Heritage Farm
2   Grimm Farm
3   Dakota City Heritage Village
4   LeDuc Historic Estate
5   Sibley House Historic Site
6   Ames-Florida-Stork House
7   Riley L. Bartholomew House
8   Charles H. Burwell House
9   George Christian Mansion
10 Cummins-Grill Homestead
11 Eidem Homestead
12 Historic Fort Snelling
13 Ard Godfrey House
14 William E. Goodfellow Mansion
15 Longfellow House Hospitality Center
16 Gideon Pond House
17 Purcell-Cutts House
18 Smith-Douglas-More House
19 John H. Stevens House
20 Swan J. Turnblad Mansion
21 J. V. Bailey House
22 Bruentrup Heritage Farm
23 Fillebrown House
24 Germanic American Institute
25 Gibbs Museum
26 The Governor's Residence
27 James J. Hill House
28 Alexander Ramsey House
29 Hooper-Bowler-Hillstrom House
30 Historic Murphy's Landing
31 Historic Stans House
32 Samuel B. Strait House
33 Erickson Log House
34 Gammelgården Museum
35 Historic Red Rock Mission Cabin
36 The Warden's House Museum
37 Woodbury Heritage House

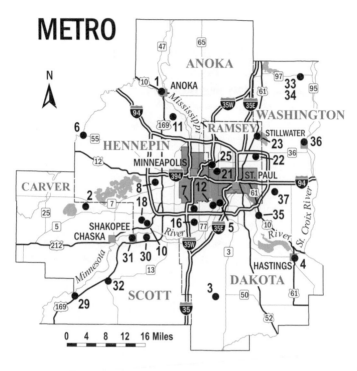

METRO

N

ANOKA

ANOKA

WASHINGTON

RAMSEY

HENNEPIN

MINNEAPOLIS

STILLWATER

CARVER

ST. PAUL

SHAKOPEE
CHASKA

HASTINGS

DAKOTA

SCOTT

0 4 8 12 16 Miles

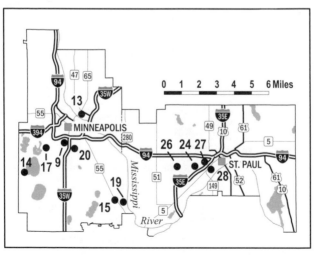

MINNEAPOLIS

0 1 2 3 4 5 6 Miles

ST. PAUL

ANOKA COUNTY

1. ANOKA COUNTY HERITAGE FARM

Anoka County Fairgrounds, 3200 St. Francis Boulevard, Anoka. Anoka County Historical Society, 763-421-0600; Anoka County Suburban Fair, 763-427-4070

The Old Farm Place, as it is known, comes to life for a week each year during the Anoka County Fair, usually held in late July. At the center of the village is a white, wood-frame farmhouse furnished in the style of the 1930s–40s. Volunteers demonstrate household chores using early equipment and wash laundry using lye soap and a wringer washer in the farmhouse's detached summer kitchen. An original log barn houses farm animals during the fair.

Also open to visitors at the site are a post office, an early schoolhouse from Andover, a 1900 jail from Burns Township, the 1893 Constance Free Church, and a blacksmith shop staffed with smithies repairing metal objects.

The Anoka County History Center and Library, located in the former Anoka City Library, features local historical displays as well as special programs and events throughout the year.

CARVER COUNTY

2. GRIMM FARM 〔NR〕

Carver Park Reserve, Victoria, near Lowry Nature Center. 763-694-7650

Wendelin and Julianna Grimm immigrated from Kusheim, Germany, to Carver County in 1857. In 1859 Grimm purchased and began farming eighty acres of land with alfalfa seeds brought from Germany. After farming for many years, Grimm died in 1890 in Chaska.

In 1900 University of Minnesota Professor Willet

Grimm Farm, Carver Park Reserve, Victoria

Hays, breeder and founder of the American Genetic Association, "discovered" the alfalfa that Grimm had cultivated. Grimm's alfalfa is credited as the first strain of winter-hardy alfalfa grown in the United States, and in 1924 a commemorative plaque placed on a large boulder at the farmstead noted the birthplace of the famous strain.

Grimm's farmhouse was occupied until the 1950s. In 1962 Hennepin County's parks board purchased the farm, which was designated a state historic site. In 1974 the farmhouse was added to the National Register of Historic Places for its significance in agricultural history.

This L-shaped house, built of cream-colored Chaska brick in 1875–76, has a kitchen, parlor, and two bedrooms on the main floor. The original portion of the house features front and rear gables with chimneys at each end. Four symmetrical windows on the front façade have two-over-two panes of glass and arched window openings.

Entering the house through the kitchen, visitors will find an assortment of early kitchen utensils. The parlor has an Eastlake-style settee and chairs, a parlor stove, and an 1870s Eastlake pump organ. An exhibit display includes historical photos of the Grimm family and the farm. The house has four bedrooms upstairs and a room above the kitchen, which at one time served as a chicken coop.

The Carver County Historical Society and the Three Rivers Park District jointly maintain and operate the house and historic farmstead.

DAKOTA COUNTY

3. DAKOTA CITY HERITAGE VILLAGE
Dakota County Fairgrounds, 4008 Two-Hundred-Twentieth Street, Farmington. 651-460-8050

This recreated early-twentieth-century village includes twenty-two buildings. The village comes to life during the county fair in August, when costumed interpreters demonstrate village activities during living-history events. The modern museum showcases Dakota County history, especially agriculture and rural life, with a display of tractors and other farm equipment.

Dakota City has two parallel streets and one bisecting street. The village includes an operating blacksmith shop, newspaper office, and photography studio. Some buildings are original structures moved to the site, while others are recreated or reused structures.

Dakota City Heritage Village, Farmington

Original structures include the 1902 Eureka Township one-room school, the 1867 Vermillion Presbyterian Church, the 1860s railroad depot from Dahlgren Township in Carver County, the 1904 brick Randolph jail, and the 1918 brick Vermillion State Bank. The 1903 Gibson barbershop is from the village of Rosemount, and a fully stocked general store is housed in an 1869 building moved here from Lakeville.

The 1892 Harris House, moved from Lakeville Township, is a white, wood-frame farmhouse. On the grounds is an heirloom garden cared for by the Lakeville Garden Club.

Adaptive reuse of historic structures includes the photography studio, which is located in the former 1861 Vermillion Township school. The library is located in the 1938 Trinity Lutheran Church from Farmington, the Land and Law Office in the 1870s school from Lebanon Township, and the Dakota City village hall in the 1869 New Trier town hall. The harness and blacksmith shops are also original nineteenth-century buildings. New structures include the Dakota City post office, the Dakota City Free Press, the dressmaker's shop, and the fire barn.

Special events include a Wild West weekend in the fall, Grand History Days in October, and the Village Christmas in December. During the county fair in August, the village features carriage tours, costumed interpreters, and the Dakota Chautauqua, a musical theater production about Dakota County history.

4. LeDUC HISTORIC ESTATE 🔳
1629 Vermillion Street (Highway 61), Hastings, south of downtown Hastings. 651-552-7548 or 651-437-7055

The LeDuc Historic Estate, also known as the LeDuc-Simmons House, opened to the public in 2005. The house is nationally significant because of its unaltered Gothic Revival architecture, based on an original Andrew Jackson Downing design. Mary (Bronson) LeDuc chose the design from Downing's *Cottage Residences*, an architectural plan book first published in 1842. The house survives virtually unaltered since its completion in 1865–66.

William Gates LeDuc hired one of St. Paul's first practicing architects, Augustus F. Knight, to draw up the working plans for their house based on Downing's design. Architect Abraham M. Radcliff later created a more complete set of plans based on Knight's drawings. The $30,000 mansion was built between 1861 and 1865, while LeDuc served in the Civil War and the family stayed in Ohio. In 1865 LeDuc and his wife and children returned to their not-quite-finished house.

LeDuc was a pivotal leader in the early history of the state, a general in the Civil War, and a leader involved in early railroad developments. From 1877 to 1880 he served as the US Commissioner of Agriculture under President Hayes, and the family moved for a time to Washington, D.C.

The family eventually sold the property to antique dealer Carroll Simmons, who deeded ownership of the property to the Minnesota Historical Society in 1958 with the stipulation that he be able to continue using the house for his business. The LeDuc House was added to the National Register of Historic Places in 1970.

Restoration with state funding began in 2003 and was completed in 2005, when the city of Hastings assumed ownership. The Dakota County Historical Society manages the historic site, installs exhibits, and schedules public events.

Visitors, who now enter the house through the rear entrance, are brought outside to view the front face of the fifteen-room Gothic Revival mansion. The house has a central entrance in the tower, which extends out from the façade, two large verandahs, elaborately carved bargeboards, and finely crafted stonework. Inside, on the left side of the hallway, is the parlor featuring displays highlighting the rich history of the home, family, and area. Across the hall is the library and, behind that, the dining room. The back corner room, across from the dining room, was the original kitchen.

Visitors are taken to tour the carriage house and view the recreated historic orchard where LeDuc experimented with growing apples in Minnesota's northern climate. The original carriage house was modeled after one in the Downing plan book that was first built for the founder of Vassar College in New York. Inside the carriage house are exhibits and historical artifacts telling the story of a former slave, George Daniels, who lived in the carriage house and worked for the LeDucs after the war.

Visitors return to the main house and ascend the staircase to tour the second-story bedrooms, including daughter Minnie's room, now used as a gift shop. The LeDuc grounds include a strolling woods, heirloom apple orchard, grapery, peony garden, and ancient oak trees. Special events take place at the estate throughout the year, including a Civil War weekend held the first weekend in June.

5. SIBLEY HOUSE HISTORIC SITE 🅼 ℝ
1357 Sibley Memorial Highway (State Highway 13), Mendota. 651-452-1596

The Sibley House Historic Site contains a cluster of original buildings, including Henry H. Sibley's stone house. Two families, the Faribaults and the Sibleys, made their mark at this site. Jean Baptiste Faribault first operated a trading post here in 1819, joined in 1826 by the competing American Fur Company. Henry Hastings Sibley came to manage the company in 1837. In 1849 Sibley's house became the temporary territorial headquarters while Governor Alexander Ramsey and his family were guests of Sibley. The first territorial court was held here at Mendota.

The seven structures that remain at the site include the Sibley and Faribault Houses, which were built in a blend of the Federal–Greek Revival styles using limestone quarried in St. Peter, Minnesota. The other structures include Hypolite Dupuis's 1854 house, an 1854 summer kitchen, an 1839 powderhouse, and an 1843 cold store building.

The Daughters of the American Revolution sponsored the restoration, and the Sibley House opened to the public as a museum in 1910. The Mendota Historic District, including the existing buildings and the nearby church, was added to the National Register of Historic Places in 1970. The Sibley House was added to the National Register of Historic Places in 1972. In 1997 the Minnesota DAR turned ownership of the Sibley Historic Site over to the Minnesota Historical Society, which now operates the site.

Tours depart from the 1854 Dupuis House, which was built of brick from Milwaukee, Wisconsin. The first stop on the tour is the 1843 cold store, now recreated as a trading post with furs, beads, cloth, and other goods.

Sibley's 1836 limestone house was built by Swiss-German mason John Mueller. The two-and-one-half-story house, which is in various states of restoration, contains many original artifacts from the Sibleys. It is the oldest remaining private house in Minnesota.

A square portico forms the front entrance. The windows feature exterior shutters with stone lintels and sills.

Inside the Sibley House, a long hall divides the front parlor from the rear kitchen, dining room, and office on the main floor. The upper floors contain the family bedrooms and nursery, which are furnished with family artifacts. The parlor contains a melodeon, secretary, and horsehair-covered chairs. In the dining room, the Sibleys' china rests in the built-in china cabinets, while their monogrammed linens grace the set table. Henry Sibley's office is filled with some of his treasured artifacts, including his walnut desk, top hat, and powder horn.

Next door is Jean Baptiste Faribault's 1840 home, otherwise known as the Faribault Hotel. In 1854, Jean Baptiste moved to Faribault, Minnesota, to live with his son, while his grandson George and his wife Euphrasine operated the hotel until 1870.

The main floor of the Georgian-style Faribault House consists of a long room for billiards and a bar, a dining room, and the bedroom, all separated by a central hall with front and rear entry doors. With a similar layout, the upper floor originally housed the inn's sleeping rooms, but now displays information about the US-Dakota War of 1862 and military artifacts, including Sibley's 1865 uniform and nineteenth-century firearms.

Themed teas, special events, and family days are held often, and on June 23, the Fête de la St. Jean-Baptiste celebrates Quebecois French heritage. The site also hosts a fur trade encampment and reenactment.

HENNEPIN COUNTY

6. AMES-FLORIDA-STORK HOUSE ⬚
8131 Bridge Street, Rockford, near State Highway 55.
763-477-5383

The Ames-Florida-Stork House Museum is operated through a joint effort of the city of Rockford and the Rockford Area Historical Society. The Greek Revival house was added to the National Register of Historic Places in 1979.

In 1860 George Ames, a founder of Rockford, began building this house as a retirement home. With Guilford George and his brother-in-law, Joel Florida, Ames created the development company that established the town of Rockford and operated the Rockford Woolen Mills, the Florida Flour Mills, and others.

The house was built with wood lumbered and milled entirely at their sawmill. The butternut wood used in the interior trim was cut from the property. This unique structure has a sprawling layout that includes additions from subsequent owners. The summer kitchen and barn are connected to the house. The house features white, wooden siding and shutters on the six-over-six windows. The long gallery of the first- and second-story porches covers the front façade of the house.

The Ames-Florida-Stork House stands as an example of more than one hundred years of life in rural Minnesota. The museum tells the stories of the lives of three of Rockford's most prominent families from 1862 to 1983. The museum displays a collection of nineteenth- and early-twentieth-century furnishings, and the historical society maintains a sizeable vintage clothing collection.

Today, the rooms of the house reflect different time periods and different owners. The dining room is from the 1940s, when the Stork family lived there. The music room features butternut woodwork, which is found throughout the house. The Florida family added the dining room and the kitchen in the late-nineteenth century. The parlor has changed little since the Ames family built the house. The ground floor "sky parlor" retains the original wallpaper from the Florida family in the early-twentieth century.

Yearly events include a children's chore day in October, candlelight evening tours on Halloween, and a Christmas tea.

7. RILEY L. BARTHOLOMEW HOUSE Ⓝ

6901 Lyndale Avenue South, Richfield, at Sixty-Ninth Street.
612-798-6140

In 1852–53, General Riley Lucas Bartholomew built this Federal style residence that is now operated by the Richfield Historical Society. Bartholomew arrived in Minnesota and filed an eighty-acre claim on the shores of Wood Lake before his wife, Fannie, and children joined him here in the spring of 1853.

Born in Ohio in 1829, Bartholomew attained the rank of general in the Ohio militia. In what would become Richfield, he served as a justice of the peace, a member of the 1857 Republican Constitutional Convention, and a state senator. Bartholomew was active in the

Richfield Methodist Church, and in 1854 he also helped build the first community schoolhouse with his brother-in-law, Cincinnatus Gregory.

Bartholomew first built a two-story section of the house, then added to it two existing single-story buildings, moved from near Minnehaha Falls. The limestone foundation was quarried nearby, and the floors are made of native northern white pine. The additions to the house create varying floor and ceiling heights in the dwelling.

Visitors enter the house from a side porch. The rooms are furnished with donated artifacts and period furnishings. Visitors tour the kitchen, dining room, front hall, parlor, and three bedrooms filled with period furniture and artifacts, including a child-sized Eastlake bed filled with early dolls and other children's toys.

The Richfield Historical Society, formed in 1967 to preserve the Bartholomew home, restored it and interprets farm life in the 1850s for visitors. The house was added to the National Register of Historic Places in 1978. The new Richfield History Center opened in 2005.

8. CHARLES H. BURWELL HOUSE [NR]
13209 East McGinty Road, Burwell Park, Minnetonka, at County Highway 5 (Minnetonka Boulevard). 952-939-8200

Charles Henry Burwell managed the Minnetonka Mill Company from 1874 to 1884. He bought land from the mill company and completed his house on it in 1883. This Italian villa home, now operated by the city of Minnetonka and the Minnetonka Historical Society, is probably modeled after plans found in Palliser's American Cottage Home catalog.

Burwell married his second wife, Mary Carey Dunham, in 1876. They had two children, Louise and Loring. In 1958 Louise sold the house to the William J. Smith family, and the city of Minnetonka bought the house from the Smith estate. The house was added to the National Register of Historic Places in 1974. The historical society operates the house as a museum. The property contains an attached woodshed, one of the fifteen original worker cottages, and the 1894 mill office, which now displays artifacts from the Minnetonka area.

Charles H. Burwell House, Minnetonka

Visitors enter the dwelling from the back into the kitchen. A narrow rear kitchen stairway leads to the second floor. Visitors view the room used by the hired help, a bathroom, the children's rooms, and a guestroom that looks out over the front of the house. Visitors then take the staircase down to the front vestibule. A door leads to the Burwells' bedroom, with another door to the front parlor. The dining room is wallpapered in a stunning gilded Eastlake pattern.

Yearly events include the February Kids Fest, May Day, a Christmas open house, and an ice cream social in June.

9. GEORGE CHRISTIAN MANSION

2303 Third Avenue South, Minneapolis, south of Franklin Avenue. 612-870-1329

George Henry Christian worked with the Washburn-Crosby Flour Milling Company and built his house just across Fair Oaks Park from the Washburn residence. The home is now the Hennepin History Museum operated by the Hennepin County Historical Society.

Construction on the house began in 1916 using a design by Minneapolis architects Hewitt and Brown. When Christian died in 1918, his son, George Chase Christian, and daughter-in-law, Caroline Knight Christian, continued the work. Caroline completed the

L-shaped house in 1920 at a cost of more than $100,000. Living there until 1956, she donated the building to the Minneapolis Institute of Arts, which sold it to the historical society in 1957. The society uses the home for its museum, research library, and archives.

The English Renaissance Revival home resembles a castle with balustraded cornices. A bay window with Tudor rose-patterned stone exterior ornaments overlooks the park. The home originally had five bedrooms, an upstairs sitting room, a library and music room, dining room, conservatory, kitchen, butler's pantry, servants' quarters, and storage rooms. The main door features a wrought-iron grillwork panel designed by master ironsmith Samuel Yellin, with swirls of leaves and vines in circle, square, and fleur-de-lis patterns that also appear in the main stairway railings. The entrance door opens onto a cavernous hallway with carved floral trellis patterns in the domed stone ceiling. The lower level of the foyer has bathrooms and the original billiard room, which now serves as the museum's reading room.

The library and music room had a raised stage for musical entertainment. This room features burled African cypress floors, wainscoting, carved woodwork and moldings crafted from walnut, and an impressive imported English stone fireplace with carved acanthus-leaf designs.

The dining room was designed with an oriental influence and originally featured metallic gold-paneled walls, Persian rugs, and a pair of Chinese lacquered cabinets flanking the hand-carved Carrera-marble fireplace. The floors and paneling are crafted from oak. The room now features exhibits about the history of Hennepin County and its people. A door from the dining room leads to the original butler's pantry, flower arranging room, and kitchen. This area is currently used for archival storage of rare books and documents.

The second-story master bedroom and guestrooms now serve as exhibition galleries. These rooms feature original woodwork, paneling, and marble fireplaces.

Mrs. Christian's personal sitting room contains a large bay window overlooking the historic park, originally the gardens of the Washburn estate.

10. CUMMINS-GRILL HOMESTEAD
13600 Pioneer Trail (County Road 1), Eden Prairie, west of Highway 212. 952-949-0915 or 952-949-8454

J. R. and Martha "Mattie" (Clark) Cummins bought this farm just south of Staring Lake in Eden Prairie in 1856. They lived in the brick house built in 1879–80 until 1908. Cummins was a horticulturist involved in the establishment of the Minnesota Horticultural Society. The house is now owned by the City of Eden Prairie and operated by the Eden Prairie Historical Society.

Edwin and Harriet (Sprague) Phipps owned the farm from 1908 until 1934 and operated a roadside stand here. Their son-in-law and daughter, Martin and Mildred Grill, owned the farm from 1934 to 1976. Martin "Pappy" Grill had an airplane landing strip on his property, which he sold in 1943 to the American Aviation Corporation. The strip became Flying Cloud Airport, now located across the highway. The Grill family sold the farm in 1976 to the city of Eden Prairie to create a park. The John R. Cummins House was added to the National Register of Historic Places in 1982.

Cummins-Grill Homestead, Eden Prairie

This brick home has Greek Revival and Italianate elements. The wide trim in the gable end juts in with a discontinuous pattern typical of the Greek Revival style, and the use of brick and the creation of segmental arches over the windows are Italianate. The home has a gable front with a west side wing and an L-shaped front porch.

The south-side entrance of the house brings visitors into a room with a corner cabinet, a buffet, and an oval oak pedestal table with Empire Revival-style upholstered chairs. The main floor contains parlor, bedroom, bathroom, living room, and kitchen. On the second story are four bedrooms. The west side of the house contains a porch into the kitchen as well as a ground-level cellar door.

Four original wooden outbuildings and a milk house are located on the museum grounds.

11. EIDEM HOMESTEAD

4345 One-Hundred-and-First Avenue North, Brooklyn Park, off State Highway 610. 763-493-4604 or 763-493-8333

The restored John Eidem farm, owned by the family for eighty-two years, is now the Brooklyn Park Historical Farm, a living-history farm that portrays life in the early-twentieth century. In 1976 the city of Brooklyn Park obtained a federal grant to purchase the Eidem House and ten acres of land, and the museum opened in 1979.

John Eidem Jr. was born in 1869 in Brooklyn Township. In 1892 he married Electa "Lectty" Cotton, who was born in 1872 in Hennepin County. In 1894 they purchased thirty-nine acres of this farm in Brooklyn Township. Here they raised two sons, Archie and Leland.

It is believed that the earliest section of the house, built in the Upright-and-Wing style by owners Silas and Margaretha Merrill, dates to the late 1870s. Around 1905, Electa and John Eidem Jr. added on to the house on the north end, creating a blend of styles with Victorian, Queen Anne, and Italianate details. Elements presumably added on at the time included the central hipped roof, the gabled wings with the diamond-pattern and gingerbread details, and the extended dining room with bay window.

Touring visitors enter the rear of the house through a side porch into a large kitchen. This is still a farm kitchen complete with a working woodstove used during special events. The kitchen connects to a large dining room, which leads to a main hall and front parlor. Most of the donated furnishings throughout the home are from the late-nineteenth century or early-twentieth century.

The stairway to the second floor angles at a landing where there is a large picture window with decorative stained glass. Upstairs are three bedrooms, including one displayed as a sewing room and one filled with early toys.

Maintained as a working farm, the property is still home to chickens, ducks, cows, horses, sheep, goats, and pigs. There are three outbuildings, a chicken coop, windmill, and a large barn.

Special events often feature reenactors and include fall harvest festivals, Halloween 1900, Thanksgiving dessert, and an old-fashioned Norwegian Christmas.

12. HISTORIC FORT SNELLING 🏠 Ⓡ
Highways 5 and 55, east of the Twin Cities International Airport. 612-726-1171

Fort Snelling was built in the early 1820s to expel British fur traders and to exert US military influence in the area. The site is now operated by Minnesota Historical Society.

In 1819, the 5th Regiment of Infantry began to construct the fort, which was completed by 1825. Construction required the efforts of more than 300 soldiers. An estimated seventy-five to one hundred women and children also lived at the fort during this time.

The fort was originally called Fort St. Anthony. Its

Commander's House, Fort Snelling (*Jet Lowe for HABS–HAER/MHS*)

name was changed to Fort Snelling in 1824 in honor of commanding officer Colonel Josiah Snelling, who oversaw the fort's design and construction.

In the 1950s the Minnesota Historical Society began working with the state legislature to preserve the site and save the buildings from destruction. The fort was designated Minnesota's first National Historical Landmark in 1960, and the Fort Snelling Historic District was designated in 1966. The fort had been largely unused for many years, and many of the buildings were in great disrepair. Most of the restoration work was done in the 1970s.

The hexagonal-shaped South Battery, which is three stories high, was part of Snelling's original design. Other reconstructed buildings include the guardhouse, shops, sutler's store, schoolhouse, barracks, and hospital. The Round Tower is considered the oldest permanent structure in Minnesota. The stone officers' quarters, built in 1846 on 1820s stone foundations, replaced an earlier log structure.

The Commanding Officer's House, considered the oldest remaining residence in Minnesota, was used until

1946. Built between 1820 and 1824, it features smooth-cut stone on the front façade and rough-cut limestone on the side of the building. Over the years the interior and exterior of the home have been extensively remodeled. At one time the exterior was converted to the Spanish Mission style. Restoration brought the structure back to its 1824 appearance, and it is now furnished in the Federal style using Snelling's 1827 property inventory as a guide.

On either side of the house's central hall is a parlor; the north parlor is set up as the formal dining room and the south parlor as the family sitting room. At the rear of the house is Colonel and Mrs. Snelling's bedroom and, across the hall, the children's bedroom. The second story contains two large guest rooms, originally unfinished quarters. Outside, a rear staircase leads to the lower level, which contains the kitchen, where hearth cooking takes place daily. Across the hall from the kitchen is the Regimental Headquarters, which includes the colonel's private office with a replica 1820s cherry cabinet with pigeonhole storage compartments.

Historic Fort Snelling is the state's largest living-history museum. During the summer season and special events, this restored 1820s fort comes to life with costumed guides who are role-playing soldiers and civilians living and working at the fort. Throughout the day, visitors can witness musket and cannon firing demonstrations as well as other 1820s activities.

13. ARD GODFREY HOUSE

50 University Avenue NE, Minneapolis, in Chute Square Park. 612-870-8001

Ard Godfrey, a millwright from Maine, arrived in 1847 and supervised the building of the first sawmill at the Falls of St. Anthony. He built this house in 1848 with the first lumber sawed at the mill. In 1849, Harriet Godfrey and her children moved to Minneapolis to join her husband in the newly built house. The Godfrey family lived in the house from 1849 until 1852 and then moved to a larger home. Several other families lived in the house until 1905, when it was sold to the Minnesota Territorial Pioneers' Association and moved to its current site at Chute Square.

The building was used as a museum until 1934. Under sponsorship of the Woman's Club of Minneapolis in conjunction with the city of Minneapolis, the house was restored and reopened to the public in 1979.

The Ard Godfrey House is a classic one-and-one-half story Greek Revival cottage. The windows are symmetrical on the front façade, with the door in the center and a pair of windows on either side. The second-story bedrooms have windows in the side gable ends. The doorway is paneled with sidelights and framed by pilasters supporting a cornice heading.

This seemingly small house is actually quite spacious. The front door leads to an open foyer with a central staircase. On the east side is the family sitting room, and on the west side is the formal parlor with recreated wallpaper, upholstered furnishings, and a rosewood Chickering piano, similar to the one the Godfreys owned.

At the rear of the house is a dining room, which connects to the kitchen wing, a later addition now filled with period utensils and early kitchen equipment. In the west corner of the house, off the dining area, is a small bedroom. Upstairs there are three furnished bedrooms and a large storage room.

Legend tells that Mrs. Harriet Godfrey had dandelion seeds sent to her from Maine so she could grow them to eat the leaves, use the heads for wine, and make tea from the roots. Today, the lawn is kept trimmed but unmowed in the summer months to protect the dandelions. Special events include the Dandelion Days celebration in May, a Teddy Bear tea, and Christmas tours.

14. WILLIAM E. GOODFELLOW MANSION

3537 Zenith Avenue South, Minneapolis, at West Calhoun Parkway. 612-926-3878

In 1975 Earl Bakken, cofounder of Medtronic and inventor of the first wearable, transistor-powered pacemaker, created what is now the Bakken Library and Museum of Electricity and Life. It occupies William E. Goodfellow's English Tudor mansion, built between 1928 and 1930. Housed here is Bakken's unique collection of antique medical and electrical devices, which contains over 11,000 books and other historical documents, as well as 2,000 instruments and machines.

William Goodfellow was the son of R. S. Goodfellow, a successful dry goods merchant who sold his store in 1902 to George D. Dayton. Goodfellow went to Europe with his architect, Carl A. Gage, to find an architectural model for his house. An avid collector, Goodfellow returned with tapestries and other artifacts to furnish the home, which was originally one-and-one-half stories with seven bedrooms and eleven bathrooms. When Goodfellow died in 1944, he donated the house to the Girl Scouts. The mansion was eventually sold to Earl Bakken, who opened the house as a museum in 1975.

Made of stone and stucco, the English Tudor mansion looks like two different houses. The formal stone façade in front is castle-like in architecture and covered with ivy vines. It features a slate roof, leaded panes in every window, and decorative stone carvings. The servant's area at the rear of the house is more in the English Cottage style of stucco and wooden beams.

Some rooms in the house are largely unchanged. A paneled dining room is on one side of the breakfast nook. On the other side is the Great Hall, which is seventeen feet high with a beamed ceiling, a second-story balcony, oak floors, walnut paneling, and stained glass windows.

The dining room and Great Hall open onto a Turkish-style, domed hallway with red tile floors and French doors leading to gardens. Outside is the Florence Bakken Medicinal Garden. The lovely garden has a pond with a bronze statue of Mercury in the center.

The new wing, built in 1999 in the original home's basement, juts out as the property slopes down toward Lake Calhoun. The museum features interactive displays utilizing early electrical instruments. The museum's "Frankenstein: Mary Shelley's Dream" exhibit recreates Dr. Frankenstein's laboratory.

15. LONGFELLOW HOUSE HOSPITALITY CENTER

4800 Minnehaha Avenue, Minnehaha Falls Park, Minneapolis. 612-230-6520

In 1907 Robert "Fish" Jones built this house on the west side of Minnehaha Falls Park. Jones was an entrepreneur who created the Longfellow Gardens Botanical and Zoological Park. A Minneapolis legend, he was an eccentric in the truest sense. The zoo was filled with exotic animals, and a small railway circled the perimeter of the gardens.

The house is a two-thirds-size replica of Henry Wadsworth Longfellow's home in Cambridge, Massachusetts,

Longfellow House Hospitality Center, Minneapolis

one of four known "copies" of this famous house. Jones's replica features exterior ornaments typical of the mid-Georgian architecture of the original house, although on a reduced scale. The symmetrical design features sun-porch wings on the north and south sides and four Ionic pilasters attached to the front face of the house.

Jones sold the house in 1936 to the Minneapolis Park Board, which used it as a library, a warming house for a nearby ice skating rink, and later as a "haunted house" for Halloween celebrations. In 1994 the house was relocated and restored, and in 2001 it opened to the public. The Longfellow House Restoration Group fought to save the structure, and the Kodet Architectural Group is responsible for the adaptive-reuse renovation.

The house is now a hospitality and interpretive center for the Grand Rounds Scenic Byway, the fifty-mile tour of Minneapolis's scenic lakes and riverfront. Visitors can pick up a byway map, view changing art exhibits, and see historical photos of Minnehaha Park.

The interior of the house has been renovated to meet today's needs. A sofa and lounge chairs surround the fireplace in the north parlor. The south sunroom features a hand-painted mural depicting animals from the Longfellow zoological gardens. Photographs of early Minneapolis are displayed throughout the house.

16. GIDEON POND HOUSE 🏠

401 East One-Hundred-Fourth Street, Bloomington, between Portland and Nicollet Avenues. 952-563-8693

Tucked into a quiet, wooded area in Bloomington is the homestead of Gideon Hollister Pond and his family. Gideon and his brother, Samuel, arrived in Minnesota in 1834 to become missionaries to the area's native peoples. The brothers worked at encampments of Little Crow's band at Kaposia, now South St. Paul, and with Cloud Man's band near what is now Lake Calhoun in Minneapolis. In 1843 Gideon constructed a log house here, which served as the first church in the Bloomington area. In 1852 he built a one-story frame house and then, in 1856, the two-story brick house, which was attached to the front of the frame house. In 1910 the frame house portion was demolished.

Gideon Pond House, Bloomington

The brick house was added to the National Register of Historic Places in 1970, and Pond family members lived here continuously until 1991. In 1992, the property was given to the city of Bloomington. Today family descendents are active in the preservation and interpretation of the house museum. In 1995–96 a restoration effort began as a joint project between the Minnesota Historical Society and the city of Bloomington.

The cube house is in the Federal style, built with bricks that were manufactured on site. The house's windows are original and include shutters on the front façade of the house. The house has the typical hipped roof of the period, with a front recessed doorway with sidelights. The house has a door on each side, creating uniformity in design.

Today, visitors enter the house through the recreated one-story dwelling at the rear. Stairs lead into the family sitting room in the main house, which is furnished with family artifacts and other donated pieces. Gideon crafted the large china hutch, complete with a secret lift-up compartment at the top. There is a copy of the title to the property from 1856 signed by President Franklin Pierce.

The many doors in this room lead to the sitting room, basement, second floor used by the children, front hall, and front parlor. In the parlor is a carved oak pump organ similar to the Pond family's original organ. Across the hall is Gideon's study, with a wall of glassed-in bookcases and an upright desk built by Gideon.

On the grounds of the house is a canvas tipi that pays homage to Pond family's close connection with the Dakota. Across from the house is a garden of native plants and flowering annuals with a split rail fence. The grounds of the museum contain self-guided walking trails that focus on the native plants and their use by the Native Americans and early settlers. The museum holds a yearly Rendezvous in September, and monthly tours often feature a family activity or guest speaker.

17. PURCELL-CUTTS HOUSE [NR]
2328 Lake Place, Minneapolis, near Hennepin Avenue South.
612-870-3131 or 888-642-2787 (ext. 6323)

The Purcell-Cutts House is a nationally significant example of Prairie School architecture. William Gray Purcell and his partner George Grant Elmslie designed this 1913 home for Purcell's own family. The house was sold in 1919 to Anson B. and Edna Cutts. In 1985 their son Anson Cutts Jr. bequeathed the property to the Minneapolis Institute of Arts, which restored and then opened the house as a museum in 1990. The house was added to the National Register of Historic Places in 1974.

In 1907, with former Cornell classmate George Feick Jr., Purcell established the Minneapolis firm of Purcell and Feick. In 1910 Elmslie joined the firm. Purcell was the principal architect, Feick the design engineer, and Elmslie the artist of stunning ornamentation. Together the architects produced over seventy commissions, as well as scores of unrealized projects. They built a wide variety of residences, twenty-one banks, and structures for the industrial, civic, and commercial architectural markets.

The Purcell-Cutts house is a Prairie School showpiece. The long, narrow house was built on a 150-by-50-foot residential lot. The two-story, open-plan house features Elmslie's art glass in every window, custom stenciling throughout the house, and furnishings designed by Purcell and Elmslie (today, replicas take their place).

At night the house's eighty leaded-glass windows gleam when inside lights are turned on.

Visitors enter the elevated lot via steps from the main sidewalk. A small pool in front of the house can be seen from the front walk. Inside, a few steps lead to the sunken living room with a wall of stained glass windows, fireplace with carved wood and painted mural, and Mrs. Purcell's built-in desk. A few steps up take visitors to the elevated level containing the dining room with built-in storage cabinets and French doors, a well-designed and utilitarian kitchen, and the screened-in living porch, Purcell's specialty.

Off the landing between the first and second floors is a door to the maid's room, now used as a caretaker's room. The guestroom on the left is unique in its clever arrangement of a sink and a mirror tucked into an unassuming closet. The large master bedroom suite includes an east-facing morning room, the bedroom itself, and a sleeping porch.

The museum holds special tours throughout the year and is decorated for Christmas tours in December.

18. SMITH-DOUGLAS-MORE HOUSE
8107 Eden Prairie Road, Eden Prairie. Coffeehouse, 952-934-0145; 952-949-0915 or 952-949-8454

Today the Smith-Douglas-More House houses both a Dunn Brothers Coffeehouse and the Eden Prairie Historical Society's historical displays and meeting rooms. This unique adaptive reuse of a historic early home preserves the house and shares it with the public. The building opened in its new use in 2002.

In 1877 Sheldon Smith built this house at the approximate price of $3,500. The upstairs bedrooms were rented overnight to railway passengers. The house then passed to the Douglas family and, later, to Earl More, who worked to preserve the house and open it to the public.

The food and coffee area is located in a new rear ad-

Smith-Douglas-More House, Eden Prairie

dition to the home that replaces a dilapidated kitchen. Newly landscaped grounds include a pergola-covered patio area. An early farm building is also located behind the house. Patrons of the coffeehouse have full reign of the house to sit in the overstuffed chairs and peruse the home's historical displays. The front parlor, furnished with a Queen Anne buffet, modern sofas, and stuffed chairs, features a bay window with custom stained-glass panels created by Earl More. One former second-story bedroom is furnished with an Eastlake settee found in the attic and restored by More. The set presumably belonged to the Smith-Douglas family.

19. JOHN H. STEVENS HOUSE
4901 Minnehaha Avenue South, Minneapolis, in Minnehaha Park. 612-722-2220

Colonel John Harrington Stevens built this house in 1849–50, and it is now recognized as the first permanent homestead on what became the west bank of Minneapolis. Stevens worked as a clerk for Franklin Steele at Fort Snelling. Mr. Stevens was called by his peers the "Father of Minneapolis."

In the years 1850–55 this house became the civic

and social hub for meetings to organize both Minneapolis and Hennepin County, as well as the first state fair. In 1852 settlers gathered here to name Minneapolis and to plat and name its streets. The building served as Minneapolis's city hall until 1854.

In the 1890s a *Minneapolis Journal* reporter located the house and started a campaign to preserve it. In 1896 schoolchildren collected pennies to mount the house on wheels for relocation, and on May 28, the mayor stopped city activities so that 7,000 children, in teams, could help pull the house to Minnehaha Falls Park from the Cedar-Riverside area (see photo, p. xv).

The house sat vacant until the 1980s. Schoolchildren helped move the house again to its present site in the park in 1983. The Junior League of Minneapolis, in cooperation with the Minneapolis Parks and Recreation Board, restored the Stevens House to its original appearance, and the house opened to the public in 1985.

Today the home resides in a picturesque corner of Minnehaha Park. A picket fence surrounds it, where it is sheltered beneath a grove of ancient oak trees. The grounds feature a heritage garden with heirloom vegetables, herbs, and wildflowers. A statue of Colonel John H. Stevens is located near the walkway leading to the house.

The one-and-one-half-story Greek Revival wood-frame house has a porch along the front face of the kitchen wing. The house's simple front door opens into a formal parlor. All the furnishings in the home date from the 1840s–50s and match what Stevens would have had in his home, including the donated Chickering square pianoforte and Mr. Stevens's own Seth Thomas clock and tabletop desk.

A formal parlor adjoins the central family sitting room. The kitchen is in a separate wing reached by a step down from the central parlor. A narrow staircase off the central parlor leads to the two former bedrooms upstairs. This area has an exhibit of photos of showing the process of moving and restoring the house.

20. SWAN J. TURNBLAD MANSION, AMERICAN SWEDISH INSTITUTE

2600 Park Avenue, Minneapolis, at Twenty-Sixth Street.
612-871-4907

This castlelike, thirty-three-room mansion was built between 1903 and 1908 for $1.5 million, a huge sum of money at the time. Minneapolis architects Christopher A. Boehme and Victor Cordella created the castle out of Indiana lime-

Swan J. Turnblad Mansion, Minneapolis

stone in a Chateauesque style. The building, which is operated by the American Swedish Institute, was added to the National Register of Historic Places in 1971.

Swan J. Turnblad left Sweden at age eight with his family and grew up in Vasa, Minnesota. He became wealthy publishing the Swedish language newspaper *Svenska Amerikanska Posten,* the nation's largest Swedish American newspaper.

In 1883 Turnblad married Christina Nilsson, and their daughter, Lillian Zenobia, was born in 1884. The Turnblad family lived in this castle home for less than ten years, soon moving to an apartment across the street. In 1929 Turnblad donated his home, newspaper, personal artifacts, and an endowment for the creation of a cultural institute, originally called the American Institute of Swedish Arts, Literature, and Science. It is the oldest museum of Swedish American culture and history in the United States.

The Turnblad mansion features turrets, catwalks, spires, pinnacles, and gables similar to those found in European castles. Herman Schlink of Winona was one of the master stonecarvers responsible for the exterior artistry. The central hipped roof has many gables, and the central entrance features an extended portico with an arched opening.

The main entrance of the mansion leads to the two-story Grand Hall paneled in African and Honduran mahogany and topped by an ornately carved balcony on the second level. Ulrich Steiner, originally from Switzerland, was one of the many master woodcarvers who detailed the interior of the home. Original rooms on the main level include the salon, dining room, breakfast room, music room, and a den. The lavish interiors are highlighted by plaster ceiling moldings and woodcarvings in the wall paneling.

Climbing the wide staircase off the Grand Hall to the second floor, guests view the mammoth stained glass "Visby Window" above the landing. The Neumann and Vogel Glass Company in Stockholm recreated the painting in Swedish-made stained glass in 1908.

The mansion formerly housed family bedrooms on the second floor and the grand ballroom and servants' quarters on the third floor. These areas now hold changing exhibits of Swedish and Swedish American artwork, glassware, and folk art. The basement level of the home has been turned into a *Bokhandel* (bookshop) and *Kaffestuga* (coffee shop).

The institute offers classes ranging from Swedish language to dancing, fiddling, and painting. Events include Midsommar in June, St. Lucia's Day in early December, and Christmas holiday tours.

RAMSEY COUNTY

21. J. V. BAILEY HOUSE
Minnesota State Fairgrounds, 1263 Cosgrove Avenue, Falcon Heights. 651-632-2621

In 2006 the Minnesota State Fair Foundation unveiled a restored house on the fairgrounds. This 1912 American foursquare house was first used as a residence for Minnesota State Agricultural Society Board members while the State Fair was in session. Beginning in 1916 and continuing through 2004, this house was the year-round home for the fair's greenhouse superintendent.

The greenhouse residence has been renamed the J. V. Bailey house to honor John Vincent Bailey Jr., who founded Bailey Nurseries in 1905. Although Bailey never lived in the house, he was an early pioneer in the Minnesota nursery industry and was also a member and president of the State Fair Board during the 1920s and 1930s.

The State Fair Foundation, organized in 2001 to preserve the historic fairgrounds, is involved in several restoration efforts including landscaping, reforestation, and building preservation. The Bailey Nurseries Foundation and the Gordon and Margaret Bailey Foundation funded a large part of the restoration of the house and landscaping of the grounds.

The house has been restored with an enclosed front porch and modern updates. It features large front and rear dormers in the hipped roof, as well as Colonial Revival details. This historic greenhouse residence is one of the last remaining homes on the fairgrounds. The house will hold the fair archives, display historical exhibits, and provide public meeting space and headquarters for the foundation.

On the main floor is the former living room and an office with a golden oak desk and chair. The dining room runs the length of the north side of the house and contains a large farmhouse table for community meetings. This room displays vintage state fair posters and other artifacts. The home's second story contains offices. The rear of the house connects to the fairground greenhouses.

22. BRUENTRUP HERITAGE FARM
2170 East County Road D, Maplewood,
east of White Bear Avenue. 651–249–2100

The original Bruentrup farm was established in 1891, when William Bruentrup married Ida Wagner and her

Bruentrup Heritage Farm, Maplewood

family gave them forty acres of land as a wedding gift. The couple first built a small wood-frame house on this property. The large dairy barn and silo were built in 1905, and a brick farmhouse was added around the original home's structure in 1912.

The Maplewood Area Historical Society organized in 1997 to save the house. The Bruentrup family was involved in the setting up of the society and is still involved in its work. With private donations, the Bruentrup family's support, and grants from the Minnesota Legislature, enough money was raised to move the buildings to a new site. This thirty-two-acre plot of land was purchased in 1991 by the city of Maplewood to preserve green space. The Bruentrup Heritage Farm covers two-and-one-half acres of this site, and the rest of the property is restored prairie. The barn and some of the remaining outbuildings were moved, as was the house. Original buildings on the new farmstead site include the granary, milk house, and a tin machine shed.

The modified American Foursquare brick farmhouse has two third-story gabled dormers on the hipped roof and windows capped with brick segmental arches. The originally separate front porch and kitchen porch feature exposed decorative rafter tails.

Visitors enter the rear porch and step into the large kitchen, which was modernized in 1991, and move into the dining room. The original oak trim on the main floor is still intact, as is the large built-in oak buffet.

Special events include teas, a family fun day in June, a Johnny Appleseed event in August, and a Christmas open house.

23. FILLEBROWN HOUSE Ⓝ
4735 Lake Avenue, White Bear Lake, near US Highway 61.
651-407-5327

The Fillebrown House, often called the "Red Chalet," is operated by the White Bear Lake Historical Society. An example of the Stick architectural style, the wood-frame house is red, with green trim on the decorative crossbeams. The home's intricate cutout details in the peaks and in the front porch railings are Stick elements popular in the late-nineteenth century. When the house was built, White Bear Lake was a resort community, with train lines extending to the village from St. Paul.

Charles Noyes built this house in 1879 and sold it

Fillebrown House, White Bear Lake

three years later to George Young, a Minnesota supreme court justice. Jonas Fillebrown purchased the house in 1905. In the 1920s and 1930s, after Fillebrown and his wife Hallie died, their unmarried children Helen and Arthur lived year-round in the house and rented rooms to boarders. Helen and Arthur's rental income was supplemented by using the home as a nursery school and a tea room. After Helen died in 1977 and her brother died a year later, the house and its furnishings passed to the historical society. The house was added to the National Register of Historic Places as the Charles P. Noyes Cottage (Red Chalet) in 1976, but it is known locally as the Fillebrown House.

Helen Fillebrown, a concert pianist who had studied with Arthur Rubenstein in Germany, gave piano lessons on the 1866 Steinway grand piano located in the parlor. A hammered-metal chandelier here is in the Arts-and-Crafts style with amber-glass tulip shades. The parlor opens onto the front foyer, with a corner fireplace and angled staircase to the upper floor (not open to the public). The main floor bedroom holds the 1881 wedding dress of Helen's mother, Hallie Fillebrown, and original Eastlake mahogany furniture

24. GERMANIC AMERICAN INSTITUTE
301 Summit Avenue, St. Paul. 651-222-7027

This Colonial Revival house, designed by Thomas G. Holyoke, was built in 1905 for the George W. Gardner family. Gardner worked in investment banking, real estate, and insurance. George and his wife, Claribel, had two children, George H. and Truman P. Gardner.

The Gardner family lived in the house until 1948, when it was sold to the Sisters of St. Benedict. The house became known as St. Paul's Priory, and the renovated carriage house became known as St. Peter's Hall. The Volkfest Association purchased the house in 1965. Today the words *"Volksfest Kulturhaus"* appear above the front portico.

The golden Kasota limestone used for the exterior, the decorative stone quoins, and keystone lintels above the windows are a testament to the fine craftsmen who built the home. The Georgian style is prominent in the home's exterior. Details include sidelights and fanlights surrounding the front entrance, as well as a single Palladian window on the west side of the house.

The formal front hall features a vestibule with leaded glass sidelights and a dramatic central open staircase. On the main floor are three parlors, as well as the dining room, pantry, and large kitchen. The second-story bedrooms serve as history rooms with German and German American artifacts and as a research library. Works of art decorate the hallway.

The third-floor ballroom has a large Palladian window and murals painted by Gunther Walther in 1978. The mansion's basement has been turned into a *Rathskeller*, or German bar, with murals on the walls and the crests of the German states. The working bar has authentic German beer steins and glasses.

The institute hosts the *Deutsche Tage* German heritage event in June, among many other cultural events.

25. GIBBS MUSEUM OF PIONEER AND DAKOTAH LIFE 🆁

2097 West Larpenteur Avenue, Falcon Heights.
651-222-0701 or 651-646-8629

Heman and Jane De Bow Gibbs moved to Minnesota to work with Cloud Man's band of Dakota near Lake Calhoun in Minneapolis. In 1849, Gibbs acquired 160 acres of land in what is now Falcon Heights. The family lived for five years in a sod dugout and for thirteen years in a one-room house built in 1854. The 1867 addition gave the house an additional parlor and bedroom on the main floor, a front porch and formal entrance, and a full second story with four bedrooms. The Gibbses raised six children on this farm.

Operated today by the Ramsey County Historical

Society, the farmstead was added to the National Register of Historic Places in 1975. The site houses historical displays of photographs and artifacts pertaining to the Gibbs family and their property, as well as to Ramsey County history.

Visitors enter the house from the side porch door, which opens onto the original parlor of the home. The farmhouse originally consisted of this one room with a loft for sleeping. Today this room is set up as a parlor on one side with a kitchen area on the other, as it would have been when the house was first built. Many of the items on display in the house are from the Gibbs family.

Guided tours show the main floor formal parlor, small bedroom, and kitchen. The front entrance stairs lead to the family bedrooms on the second floor. A large open room, created in an 1875 addition, now houses touch-and-feel exhibits of tools and other household items. The rear room is furnished as it would have been for housing farmhands.

On the museum grounds is a 1958 red barn designed by noted Minnesota architect Edwin Lundie. Rudolph Fischer, a Gibbs family son-in-law, built the early-twentieth-century white barn. The Stoen Schoolhouse was brought to this site in 1966 from Chippewa County.

Today the property is maintained as a farm with pens of chickens and ducks, horses and cows, and sheep to pet. The farm plots are worked with vegetables, and a native prairie planting is located near the replica sod house, which is close in size to the one Heman Gibbs built.

The Gibbs Museum interprets not only pioneer farm life but the unique connection the family made with the Dakota tribes who summered on Lake Calhoun. A Dakotah Medicine Teaching Garden was created in 2003 outside the Dakotah Learning Lodge. The museum holds a spring festival in May, a country-wedding event in June, and a harvest festival in October.

26. THE GOVERNOR'S RESIDENCE [NR]
1006 Summit Avenue, St. Paul. 651-297-2161

The official residence of the governor of Minnesota was built in 1910–11 as a private home for St. Paul lawyer and lumber baron Horace Hills Irvine, his wife Clotilde McCullough Irvine, and their children. William Channing Whitney designed the three-story English Tudor dwelling. The Irvine family lived in the home from 1912 until 1965, when the Irvine daughters, Clotilde Irvine Moles and Olivia Irvine Dodge, offered the twenty-room mansion to the state to be the official residence of the governor. In 1974 the house was added to the National Register of Historic Places.

The 16,000-square-foot house has nine bedrooms, eight bathrooms, nine fireplaces, a den, a drawing room, a formal dining room, and a solarium on one-and-one-half acres of grounds. The home's exterior is brick with stone cornices and archways. The front gable entrance includes parapets and a second-story balcony.

Visitors stand in the formal hallway and take in the elaborate carvings on the mammoth oak staircase. The upper floors are the governor's family's private quarters (not open to the public). Main floor tours include the formal library, the dining room with walnut woodwork and a domed ceiling, the sunken solarium with marble floors and stone walls, and the formal parlor with mahogany paneled walls and a plaster molded ceiling with carved Tudor rose medallions. The lower level features a display of images of Minnesota's First Ladies.

All of the furnishings on the main floor belong to the home, not specific governors. The paintings are on loan from area museums and artists. The official State Seal china from Pickard has approximately two hundred place settings and is used at many special dinners. The silver service is from Tiffany & Company.

On the landscaped gardens around the property are fountains from France, made at the same foundry as the Statue of Liberty, that date to the 1850s. The house serves as the official ceremonial building for the governor and for the citizens of Minnesota.

27. JAMES J. HILL HOUSE
240 Summit Avenue, St. Paul. 651-297-2555

The 36,000-square-foot James J. Hill House is the grandfather of historic house museums in Minnesota. Built between 1888 and 1891 at the cost of over $900,000, the home has thirty-two rooms, thirteen bathrooms, twenty-two fireplaces, and a one-hundred-foot-high reception hall. This five-story home built of red sandstone sits atop a bluff on fashionable Summit Avenue.

James J. Hill was called the "Empire Builder" for his work developing the Great Northern Railway and creating a transportation empire that included shipping on the Mississippi River, the Great Lakes, and the Pacific Ocean. Along the way Hill established towns and made another fortune in land speculation. His business interests included mining, farming, and banking. Hill and his wife, Mary Mehegan, had ten children within eighteen years.

James J. Hill House, St. Paul *(MHS)*

In 1925, according to Mrs. Hill's wishes upon her death, the Hill children gave the mansion to the Archdiocese of St. Paul, which used the home for a variety of purposes. In 1961 the home was designated a National Historic Landmark. In 1966 the house was added to the National Register of Historic Places, and in 1978 the Minnesota Historical Society acquired the property and began restoration for use as a historic house museum.

James J. Hill hired the Boston architectural firm of Peabody, Stearns, and Furber to design his Richardsonian Romanesque residence. The home's exterior features hipped roofs, square cut stone, bands of three windows, and a porte-cochere with Syrian arches at the front entrance. Extending from the home's east side is a large art-gallery wing, with a bank of rooftop window skylights that can be viewed from the exterior. The home boasted the latest technology available at the time, including gas and electric lighting and central heating.

Visitors begin their tour in the reception room, and then enter the adjoining music room for a brief orientation to the story of the Hill family. Tours of the first floor include the drawing room, family breakfast room, library, den, and formal dining room with its carved mahogany woodwork and matching Renaissance Revival table, chairs, buffet, and fireplace mantle. The reception hall, used as a gathering place for parties, has stunning carved woodwork. The first floor rooms feature chandeliers, mahogany furniture, and marble fireplaces. The two-story picture gallery with skylights originally held Hill's collection of French paintings, including several by Jean-Baptiste-Camille Corot. A two-story pipe organ sits at one end of the room and a massive fireplace at the other.

Visitors ascend the grand staircase to the family area on the second floor. The west wing of the second floor had five rooms for the five daughters, and Mr. and Mrs. Hill's separate rooms are in the east wing.

On the third floor, visitors watch a video on the life of James J. Hill. Visitors can see son Walter's small bedroom. The female servants' wing here had five bedrooms and one bath.

From the hallway opposite the main staircase, visitors descend to the mansion's lowest level, which was the servants' work area. The basement has marble flooring and panels covering the lower half of the walls. Visitors here view the kitchen, a wine cellar, a male servant's bedroom, the servants' dining room and sitting room, a cold storage room, a large laundry room, and the boiler room.

Special events include lectures, concerts, art exhibitions, a Halloween ghost-story program, and the "Hill House Holidays" in December.

28. ALEXANDER RAMSEY HOUSE 🏠 ℝ
265 Exchange Street South, St. Paul, at Ramsey Street.
651-296-8760

Alexander Ramsey's fifteen-room home was built between 1868 and 1872. Ramsey, who first arrived in St. Paul in 1849, was appointed Minnesota's first territorial governor and elected the state's second governor. He also served as a US senator and the US secretary of war under President Rutherford B. Hayes.

Local architect Monroe Sheire designed the house, which is crafted of limestone quarried in Minnesota. It is built in the French Second Empire style with a distinctive mansard roof. The pairs of decorative brackets, hood molds, and bay windows are similar to those found in Italianate-style buildings. The house features a central entrance to the main portion of the house.

Ramsey and his wife, Anna Earl Jenks of Pennsylvania, arrived in Minnesota with their young son. Of their three children, only one daughter, Marion, survived to adulthood. She married Charles E. Furness in 1875, and in the early 1880s she and her children returned to live in her parents' home. Marion's two daughters Laura and Anita never married and continued to reside in the home. Upon Anita's death in 1964, the house and most of its original family furnishings and artifacts were willed to the Minnesota Historical Society. The house has been carefully restored to match photographs taken in 1884.

The Ramsey House was added to the National Register of Historic Places in 1969. By 1971 the first major restoration of the first and second floors was completed, and the home was opened for public tours. Restoration continues. Today the 1970 replica carriage house serves as a gift shop and visitors' center.

The house's main-floor rooms feature thirteen-foot ceilings, arched doorways, and hand-carved black walnut and butternut woodwork. The tall windows have arched hoods with decorative lintels, butternut shutters, and curtains. The house has pine floors throughout, covered with carpets in the formal rooms.

Large, arched, wooden double doors to the outside, paired with etched-glass interior doors, lead to the center hall that divides the house into two areas. The main floor has a reception room, family library, and dining room on the east and a large formal parlor on the west side of the house. The kitchen and service areas are in the back of the house. The reception parlor has recently been restored to its early 1870s appearance with a re-upholstered original parlor suite. Double doors connect this room to the library.

The dining room contains a Renaissance Revival sideboard, chairs, and table, set with the family's Haviland china and silver service. Across the hall, the formal parlor is forty feet long with thirteen-foot ceilings and two Bohemian crystal chandeliers. The room features an 1872 rosewood Steinway, white marble fireplaces, and a suite of Renaissance Revival furniture.

On the second floor, visitors can view Ramsey's office, four bedchambers, a bathroom originally with hot and cold running water, and a room Anna called her "snuggery," where she chatted with close friends. The third floor area originally housed the servants' rooms and, later, a nursery for the grandchildren.

Many special events take place at the house through-out the year. It is decorated for Christmas during the winter season. Family programs for older children include baking cookies in the kitchen's working wood-fired stove and trying on Victorian-style clothes.

SCOTT COUNTY

29. HOOPER-BOWLER-HILLSTROM HOUSE

410 Cedar Street North, Belle Plaine, off Highway 169 at East Court Street. 952-873-4433

Sanford Hooper built the original portion of this house in 1871. The Samuel Bowler family bought the house in 1886 and made significant additions. In 1900 the Alfred Hillstrom family acquired the house, which remained in the family until 1975. All three families were active in the business community and in development of the town. In 1975 the Belle Plaine Historical Society purchased the house as a Bicentennial project and restored portions of it. The house and the land were turned over to the city, but the site is still operated by the historical society.

The white wood-frame house was built primarily in the Greek Revival style, although the additions have other stylistic influences. Reflecting the heritage of the three families who lived here, the house is furnished in three periods—mid-nineteenth-century, late-Victorian, and early-twentieth-century.

The home's front entry leads into an office. Main floor rooms include a small parlor with double doors to the formal parlor, the dining room, a sewing room, and a large rear kitchen. From here visitors take a narrow set of stairs to the second floor. Upstairs is a small room fur-nished simply as a hired-helper's room. From the hall-way a door leads to an attached two-story outhouse, the only known one surviving in Minnesota and a rarity in the country. The back bedroom features items belonging to Judge Chatfield, who founded Belle Plaine in 1854. Other rooms include a bathroom, an open area displaying early children's items, and three bedrooms.

On the museum grounds are a carriage house museum housed in a modern barn, a large garden, a small coal shed, and a small brick smokehouse.

Seasonal events include a Christmas party, a Valentine's Day luncheon, and an August flea market.

30. HISTORIC MURPHY'S LANDING

2187 East State Highway 101, one mile east of Shakopee.
763-694-7784

Historic Murphy's Landing is a living-history museum that recreates the life of early immigrants living in the Minnesota River Valley. The wooded setting in the Three Rivers Park District stretches along the scenic river. Visitors walk from the visitor's center past the 1844 French fur trading cabin built by Oliver Faribault, the Berger and Ryan family farms, and an 1887 red brick schoolhouse to reach the recreated village of Eagle Creek. The majority of the buildings were moved here from the area, and all are authentic historic buildings in various stages of restoration.

Village buildings include the 1886 Chaska and 1880 Savage railroad depots, the 1893 Stubbs Bay town hall, the 1880 New Prague general store, a reconstructed blacksmith shop, a newspaper printing shop, the 1867 Bloomington Ferry church, a doctor's office in an 1850s limestone house, and a reconstructed millinery. A weaver, spinner, and dressmaker's shop is located in a structure built from two original 1861 log cabins.

The remaining structures are homes that portray the lives of early settlers from different ethnic groups. The two-story Graffenstadt House, built in Shakopee in 1860 using balloon-frame construction methods, has a formal parlor and a separate kitchen and living area. The Martinson House is a one-room gabled wood-frame house from Prior Lake. Irish immigrant Edward Grouke built the house, and his daughter Mary Martinson lived there. The Kahl House, with two distinct parts and two "front" doors, is typical of early home businesses. This wood-frame house, built in Mayer around 1860, is used to portray the home of a woodcarver, complete with his carving tools and unfinished projects.

On the village square is a spacious one-and-one-half-story brick house that was originally a two-room log cabin built by John O'Connor in 1865. The home's second owner added on a kitchen, pantry, and second floor bedrooms and faced the house in Shakopee bricks. Across the village square from the O'Connor House is the Atwater House. This Gothic Revival cottage home was built in 1860 in the Cedar-Riverside area of Minneapolis by Isaac Atwater, who worked as a lawyer, newspaper editor, and state supreme court judge. The one-and-one-half-story house has gingerbread trim and contains a formal parlor, dining room, kitchen, pantry, and main-floor bedroom.

The site hosts special events nearly every weekend and offers hands-on history programs for children.

31. HISTORIC STANS HOUSE
235 Fuller Street South, Shakopee, south of Highway 101.
952-445-0378

The Scott County Historical Society Museum and the adjacent 1908 Stans House are the gift to Shakopee and Scott County by Maurice H. Stans, a native son of Shakopee. Stans developed a successful public accounting career and later served as director of the US budget bureau and US secretary of commerce. The museum complex opened in 1995.

The Dutch Colonial Revival boyhood home of Maurice Stans is located on the grounds of the Scott County Historical Society Museum. Stans's father, a house painter and paper hanger, built the family home in 1908. Stans's father was also a musician and local band director, and the family was well known in the community.

The one-and-one-half-story house features a cross-gambrel roof, a popular pattern obtained from plan-book companies, as well as an open front porch, wooden siding, and cedar shingles. The entire house was furnished with antique items similar to those Stans remembered from growing up in this house.

The front door leads onto a small foyer. The main floor contains a parlor, dining room, small bedroom, and rear kitchen. A door off the dining room leads to the second story, where Stans and his siblings slept. The kitchen door leads to a plank walkway, which connects the house and the museum and leads to the landscaped gardens now cared for by the city of Shakopee.

The museum hosts Christmas and Valentine's Day teas in the home.

32. SAMUEL B. STRAIT HOUSE

19520 Highway 57, Jordan, north of US Highway 169 in the Minnesota Valley State Recreation Area. 952-445-0378

The Samuel B. Strait House is all that remains of what was once the small townsite of St. Lawrence on the Minnesota River. Samuel Burton Strait, who settled in Minnesota in 1855, lived with his second wife, son, and daughter-in-law in this house until 1890, and the house remained in the family until 1920.

Samuel B. Strait House, Jordan

St. Lawrence was one of many "paper" town sites planned in anticipation of development. Previously the site was home to Dakota villages. Strait helped develop the St. Lawrence Hotel here, which he hoped would be a hub for steamboat traffic and stagecoach travelers. A school, sawmill, and post office were built, as well as six houses, but a thriving city never materialized. In 1866 a railroad built between Jordan and Belle Plaine bypassed St. Lawrence, and Strait's dreams of a thriving city in St. Lawrence were abandoned. A fire eventually destroyed the hotel, which was bulldozed in 1958.

The Scott County Historical Society, in partnership with the Minnesota Department of Natural Resources, restored the Strait house in 2000. This limestone dwelling was built in the Greek Revival style by stonemason Lyman Noble. The home's plain front façade features window lintels and enclosed rafter ends. The front gable has a center door flanked and topped by windows. An L-shaped addition features another entrance with a small, attached porch.

The three unfurnished main floor rooms now have displays about the Minnesota River Valley settlement boom, including a copy of the original 1856 survey map of the town by Stodder and Pierson and historical photos of the early townsite and its settlers.

WASHINGTON COUNTY

33. ERICKSON LOG HOUSE [N]
Old Marine Trail North and County Road 3, Scandia.
651-433-4014 or 651-433-5972

The Washington County Historical Society operates this site, known as the Hay Lake School and Erickson Log House Museum. Called "Historic Corner," the site includes a tall granite monument describing the arrival of the first Swedish settlers in Minnesota.

The Hay Lake School, constructed of brick in 1896 and used until 1963, was added to the National Register of Historic Places in 1970. In 1974, the Washington County Historical Society purchased the log house and moved it to its present site. Johannes Erickson's Log House was added to the National Register of Historic Places in 1976.

The interior of the one-and-one-half-story log dwelling is unfinished logs, although the exterior has been covered by a traditional Swedish-style siding. The main room was used for cooking and eating. It now includes an early washing machine and a cast-iron stove. The second room is furnished as a family parlor, with a stove, spinning wheel, and a child's swinging chair. The museum grounds also include an outhouse and gardens.

34. GAMMELGÅRDEN MUSEUM
20880 Olinda Trail (County Road 3), Scandia.
651-433-5053

The Gammelgården Museum preserves this area's Swedish immigrant heritage. The eleven-acre site has six buildings, three of which are Swedish-style log buildings: the 1856 Gammel Kyrkan, which is the oldest existing Lutheran sanctuary in Minnesota; the 1868 Prast Hus, the oldest existing parsonage in Minnesota; and the 1855 Immigrant Hus, a typical log home built by Swedish immigrants. Other buildings include a 1930 *stuga* (little house), an 1879 barn, and the modern Valkommen Hus Visitor Center.

The fictional story of Kirsten, the popular American Girls doll, was set in the Scandia area, where the author did research. Today, young visitors learn about the story of Swedish immigrant children and their life in early Minnesota.

The museum offers a variety of Swedish cultural events throughout the year, including coffee parties, a lutfisk dinner, and St. Lucia's day, and services and weddings are still held in the old church during the summer.

35. HISTORIC RED ROCK MISSION CABIN
Glen Road and Eleventh Avenue, Newport, off Highway 61.
651-459-2747

This 1839 log cabin, built by Rev. Benjamin T. Kavanaugh at Red Rock Missionary Camp, is the oldest Methodist building in Minnesota. The camp started in 1837 at the Sioux village of Kaposia, now South St. Paul. Rev. Kavanaugh later moved the mission site to Red Rock on the east side of the river, just north of what is now Newport. Kavanaugh lived upstairs in this cabin with his family and used the main floor for church services on Sundays and for a school run by his wife. The cabin has been moved three times and is now located on the Newport United Methodist Church property.

The two-and-a-half-story cabin has a peaked roof, five glazed windows, and a centrally located front door. The external stairway leading to the second level is a later addition. The lower level of the cabin is furnished with church pews and a rough-hewn altar, while the upstairs living quarters contain a bed, stove, sewing machine, bookcases, and other period items.

Also on this site is the limestone boulder painted with red stripes that was once used in worship by the Sioux. The cabin was specifically built next to this rock, which glaciers had carried south from the St. Cloud area; each time the cabin was moved, the rock was moved with it.

36. THE WARDEN'S HOUSE MUSEUM 🏠
602 Main Street North, Stillwater. 651-439-5956

This 1853 limestone house, now operated by the Washington County Historical Society, was the personal residence for the warden of the Minnesota Territorial Prison. It was originally adjacent to the prison. A large stone wall and a portion of the prison's lookout tower still remain.

Wardens administering the prison lived in the residence until 1914, when the prison was moved to a new facility. After that time the home housed the deputy warden and his family. In 1941 the county historical society bought the house from the state to operate as a house museum. The building was added to the National Register of Historic Places in 1974.

The Warden's House Museum, Stillwater

The Federal-style house features eight front-facing windows and an entry portico topped with a balcony. The original house had four rooms on the main floor. The home was remodeled at least twice and has been under restoration for many years.

The double front doors lead to a central hallway with open archways that were added in an early-twentieth-century remodeling. The oak floors are accented with ribboned parquet patterns around the edge of the rooms. The north room is furnished as a formal parlor with a reed organ and piano, and it connects to what would have probably been the first family dining room, now displayed as a kitchen. The dining room, which is nearly the full width of the house, is an 1878 addition. The south side of the house has two rooms connected by an open archway. One is now the music room with a square rosewood piano from the 1850s. The front room is furnished as a family parlor, with stereopticons and other amusements.

The second floor has two large, connected rooms displayed as a master bedroom and a children's room with early toys and clothes. A large room over the added-on dining room was originally the servants' quarters. This room has lumber-industry displays and local artifacts. A small back room highlights arrowheads and bead work made by the Dakota and donated to the museum.

The museum hosts an annual open house in May, as well as teas and old-fashioned baseball games.

37. WOODBURY HERITAGE HOUSE AND GARDENS

Radio Drive and Lake Road, Woodbury. 651-430-6001

The small wood-frame cottage that now serves as the Woodbury Heritage House was built in 1870 as an addition to a log cabin owned by Frederick Raths and his wife, Sophia. German immigrants to the United States in 1853, the Rath family purchased property in Woodbury in 1866. The Stutzman family bought the home in 1903 and kept it until 1993, when they sold their farm to developers. Woodbury Community Development director Dwight Picha spearheaded the effort to save this early Woodbury house, and the Woodbury Heritage Society moved and restored the building. The front of the property is surrounded by a picket fence with an arbor gate, and a split rail fence edges the rear of the property. The heritage gardens include a butterfly garden, an herb garden, and a vintage vegetable and flower garden.

A door to the left of the entry leads to the main room of the house. The light-filled space features plain plaster walls and blue gingham curtains over the three windows. Donated furnishings include a small cast-iron cook stove and a variety of early household tools including a wooden-barreled washing machine.

Woodbury Heritage House and Gardens, Stillwater

The heritage society displays photographs of early Woodbury pioneers, early Woodbury barns, and plat maps showing the city's evolution.

Linden Hill, Little Falls

CENTRAL REGION

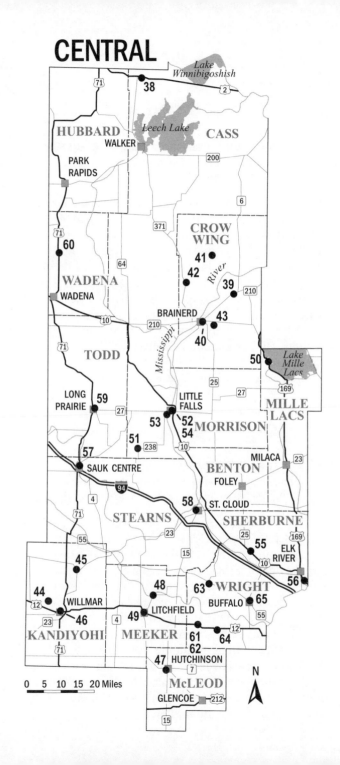

CENTRAL

Lake
Winnibigoshish

38

HUBBARD

Leech Lake

CASS

WALKER

PARK
RAPIDS

200

6

60

371

CROW
WING

41

42

River

39

210

WADENA

WADENA

64

BRAINERD

43

10

210

40

Mississippi

50

Lake
Mille
Lacs

TODD

71

169

LONG
PRAIRIE

59

25

27

MILLE
LACS

27

LITTLE
FALLS

53

52
54

MORRISON

51

238

57

10

SAUK CENTRE

BENTON

MILACA

23

94

FOLEY

4

58

ST. CLOUD

STEARNS

SHERBURNE

23

25

55

15

45

10

ELK
RIVER

169

55

56

44

48

63

WRIGHT

65

12

WILLMAR

49

LITCHFIELD

BUFFALO

46

4

61

64

KANDIYOHI

MEEKER

62

55

71

12

47

HUTCHINSON

7

McLEOD

0 5 10 15 20 Miles

N

GLENCOE

212

15

CASS COUNTY

38. LYLE'S LOGGING CAMP AND CASS LAKE MUSEUM
Lyle Chisholm Drive, Cass Lake, on US Highway 2.
218-335-6723 or 1-800-356-8615

Lyle Chisholm and his family built the log bunkhouse, wanigan, cookhouse, horse barn, file shop, and blacksmith shop that make up Lyle's Logging Camp. Chisholm worked in logging camps with his father starting at age eleven. After attending college, he worked as a forester, and at retirement he started collecting artifacts from the many abandoned logging camps in the area. He built the log cabins mostly by himself, with some help from family and friends, beginning in the early 1980s and finishing in 1995. Five log buildings are filled with logging camp items. The former Soo Line Depot across from the logging camp now serves as the Cass Lake Museum.

CROW WING COUNTY

39. CROFT MINE HISTORICAL PARK
Eighth Street North and Second Avenue East, Crosby,
north of Highway 210. 218-546-5466 or 1-800-950-2898

This seventeen-acre park uses land from the original site of the Croft Mine, which was an active underground iron-ore mine from 1916 until 1934. The Merrimac Mining Company, under the leadership of John A. Savage, began work on the Croft Mine in 1914. The historic mine site was purchased by the state of Minnesota in 1978, and the site was dedicated as a park in 1980.

The Croft Underground Mine and Historical Center has period buildings, including one remaining wood-frame house used by miners and their families. The simple, minimal furnishings are also typical. The original mine shaft is 630 feet deep, and the park offers a guided, simulated underground mining tour.

40. CROW WING COUNTY HISTORICAL SOCIETY MUSEUM

320 Laurel Street, Brainerd, west of Business Highway 371.
218-829-3268

The 1917 brick sheriff's residence and adjoining cell-block were designed by the architectural firm of Alden and Harris. Six sheriffs and their families used the residence until 1962. In 1979 a new law enforcement center replaced this building. The brick structure was added to the National Register of Historic Places in 1980 and converted into the Crow Wing County Historical Society Museum in 1983.

This two-and-a-half-story brick home features elements of the popular foursquare design mixed with the decorative elements of Dutch rowhouses and the Tudor Revival style. The parapeted gables above the front entrance and the third-story dormer have stone trim.

Inside, the downstairs hall features oak woodwork. The living room displays an assortment of furnishings from the 1920s through the 1950s, including an early radio and an early television. The dining room has a

Crow Wing County Historical Society Museum, Brainerd

built-in oak buffet and a dining room set with carved Renaissance Revival chairs. The stained glass transom windows in this room, the living room, and the porch match the floral-pattern stained glass in the buffet's cabinets. The kitchen contains the original cupboards and refinished wood floors. Prisoners' food, prepared by the sheriff's wife, was given to the jailer by means of a pass-through in one of the kitchen cabinets.

On the second story are the original family bedrooms, one of which now features early local historical items and another displays early children's toys. The matron's room was located here because of its easy access to the women's jail cells. The adjacent jail in the rear portion of the residence originally had thirteen cell blocks, four allocated for women and one which was padded.

41. HISTORIC LOG VILLAGE MUSEUM
Highway 66, Crosslake, at Highway 3.
218-692-4836 or 218-692-5400

The Historic Log Village Museum is made up of seven structures that span the area's history from logging and early settlement to the beginnings of resort-indusry tourism. The museum was established in 1980 by the Crosslake Area Historical Society.

Rufus Heath built the logger's cabin in the early-twentieth century east of Pine River, where the Heath family lived until 1928. The Ostlund Homestead Cabin was built in 1892 by August and Margaret Ostlund, who arrived in Crow Wing County from Sweden. One log cabin is now furnished as a typical tourist cabin, and the other houses have rotating historical exhibits.

A building donated to the historical society by Theron E. Dempsie has been used to recreate the Ideal Township school in Crow Wing County, which was built in 1897 and used until 1904. A replica of the 1904 Crosslake store was built on the museum grounds, and the 1923 Crosslake town hall now displays a permanent collection of area history artifacts.

Historic Log Village Museum, Crosslake

The museum's operations include a July tour, an artisan fair in August, and a candlelight tour with music and wagon rides.

42. NISSWA AREA HISTORICAL SOCIETY

25590 Main Street, Nisswa, near Highway 371.
218-963-0801

The Nisswa Area Historical Society's Log House Village Museum is located across from the city museum in the town's restored depot. The Anderson Family Charitable Trust owns the museum site, which is managed by the historical society.

The log cabins in this village were moved from the former Lumbertown USA at Madden's Resort and from the former Little Mountain Settlement in Monticello. All of the cabins are original to Minnesota and were built in the mid- or late-nineteenth century. One cabin is displayed as a German homestead, while a red frame house represents a Swedish homestead. One cabin serves as a pioneer bank, and a livery museum is located in a modern building. The village also includes the one-room Pillager School and a log summer kitchen.

The museum holds a Pioneer Day celebration in August with crafts, food, and demonstrations of early pioneer chores.

43. THIS OLD FARM AND PAUL BUNYAN LAND
17553 State Highway 18, Brainerd. 218-764-2524 or 1-877-412-4162

Richard and Marion Rademacher and their family operate This Old Farm and Paul Bunyan Land. Four generations of the family have worked to create Birch Ridge Village, located within This Old Farm, which displays Mr. Rademacher's collection of antiques, farm equipment, and old buildings. In addition to many historic buildings, the recreated village includes the newly-constructed but historic-looking train depot built for the Walt Disney movie *Iron Will*, which was filmed in the Duluth area.

The village contains a blacksmith shop, doctor and dentist offices, 1948 filling station, fire station, granary, print shop, post office, sawmill, school, shingle mill, and the Longhorn Saloon. The Sweet Shoppe has a functioning old soda fountain, an early popcorn popper, and a variety of children's toys and collectibles on display. The Red Shed is a modern building displaying the Rademachers' antiques. A restored late-nineteenth-century log house was moved from a nearby farm. It was once used as a house and a trading post, and later converted into a pig barn.

In 2003, the entire Paul Bunyan Amusement Center (including more than amusement twenty rides) was purchased by the Rademachers and relocated to This Old Farm. The twenty-six-foot-tall mechanical Paul Bunyan and his companion Babe the Blue Ox had been a fixture in Brainerd for fifty-three years.

The family holds "Show Days" in August, with demonstrations of nineteenth-century tools, chores, and crafts. In October, the fields become a haunted corn maze.

KANDIYOHI COUNTY

44. GURI AND LARS ENDRESON HOUSE 🏛

Dovre Township, Willmar, off County Road 5.
320-235-1881

The first white settlers in the area established five townships in 1856, and two years later Guri and Lars Endreson built their log cabin on the shore of Solomon Lake. The simple one-room, windowless cabin, which is preserved and operated by the Kandiyohi Historical Society, features a center front door, side door, and half-story sleeping loft.

The cabin honors Guri Endreson, known locally for her role in the US-Dakota War of 1862. After her husband and son were killed and her daughters kidnapped, Guri saved three wounded men, including the first settler of Willmar Township. The cabin was added to the National Register of Historic Places in 1986. Visitors who wish to tour the cabin need to make arrangements with the Kandiyohi Historical Society.

45. MONONGALIA HISTORICAL SOCIETY AND MUSEUM

220 Norwood Street SW, New London. 320-354-2557

The Monongalia Historical Society Museum is housed in the historic Lebanon Lutheran Church in New London, which contains county records dating to 1859. Located on the museum's grounds is the Sakariason Cabin, which is also open for viewing. Sakarias Sakariason built it in 1879 for his wife and his two sons in Irving Township. The cabin was later moved to this site. Behind the church is another cabin made of slim, rounded logs that have caulk in the cracks between them, a unique construction method in Minnesota pioneer cabins.

46. SPERRY HOUSE

228 Porto Rico Street NE, Willmar, on Business Highway 71.
320-235-1881

The 1893 Sperry House, built on Albert Henry Sperry's farm, is near the Kandiyohi County Historical Society Museum. The museum is located in the original Willmar train depot.

Sperry was a Kandiyohi farmer who had been a soldier during the US-Dakota War of 1862 and later became a prominent local official. He developed the farmland surrounding his home into a neighborhood called "Sperryville" and donated land to create Sperry Park. After Sperry died in 1917, his family lived in the house until 1970. The house was restored by the county historical society and opened to the public in 1976.

The brick house features elaborate wood moldings, stained glass, and carved oak woodwork in the interior. Decorative items and furnishings from the historical society's collections are on display in the house. A bedroom set, sewing rocker, and china service, among other items, belonged to the Sperry family.

Sperry House, Willmar

MCLEOD COUNTY

47. SCHIROO CABIN
380 North School Road NW,
Hutchinson. 320-587-2109

Schiroo Cabin, Hutchinson
(McLeod County Historical Society)

In 1879 Ferdinand Schiroo built this 26-by-20-foot log cabin in McLeod County's Round Grove Township. German immigrants Ferdinand and his wife Pauline raised eight children here. The original cabin contained a kitchen, pantry, bedroom, and loft where the children slept. In the late 1890s a living room was added.

Four generations of the Schiroo (now Schiro) family lived in this log cabin home, which is operated by the McLeod County Historical Society. Descendants donated the cabin to the society, later additions were removed, and the cabin was moved to the museum site in 1986.

Exposed floor-joist ends that support the sleeping loft and dovetailed corners are unique construction methods visible on the exterior of the cabin. The cedar-shake roof is typical of roofing materials used at the time. The original cabin had a cellar with an outside entrance and a hand-split rock foundation.

MEEKER COUNTY

48. FOREST CITY STOCKADE
66608 State Highway 24, six miles northeast of Litchfield.
320-693-6782

Forest City Stockade is a replica of the 1862 fort that provided a safe haven for settlers during the US-Dakota War of 1862. In 1976, Meeker County residents rebuilt the site as part of a Bicentennial project.

White settlers first arrived in nearby Forest City in 1856. When the US-Dakota War began in August in nearby Acton, the original stockade was constructed in one day to provide a safe haven for the surviving settlers. The stockade was attacked September 4, and fighting resulted in eight deaths. The settlers' homes were burned.

Today the rebuilt stockade stands near its original site. The center cabin is a new construction using 1860s craftsmanship and furnished with period artifacts.

To create a village atmosphere, a late-nineteenth-century log cabin was relocated on the property to be used as a replica land office, as were the authentic livery and stable building. Other buildings include candle and pottery stores, a barn, an outhouse, a windmill, and a water tower.

The August Rendezvous features reenactors who demonstrate early trades and crafts, and the stockade is also open for a pioneer Christmas event in December.

49. GRAND ARMY OF THE REPUBLIC HALL AND BLOMBERG CABIN [NR]
308 Marshall Avenue North, Litchfield, across from Central Park. 320-693-9811

This 1885 castle-like structure was built as a hall for the Grand Army of the Republic, a social organization whose members were veterans of the Union Army during the Civil War. The first Litchfield chapter of the GAR was organized in 1866. This GAR building, operated by the Meeker County Historical Society, is one of only a handful still extant in the nation, and the only completely intact hall in Minnesota. The building was added the National Register of Historic Places in 1975.

This building originally housed Frank Daggett Post #25. Daggett was a local newspaper publisher and an abolitionist who worked with John Brown. During the war he commanded two African American heavy artillery regiments. He was active in starting the GAR post in Litchfield and made sure the post was not segregated, as many of them were. The GAR post disbanded in 1949, but its sister organization, the Ladies of the GAR, continue to use the hall.

GAR Hall, Litchfield

The Meeker County Historical Society obtained the site with its full set of original meeting hall chairs and Civil War photographs of each original member. The organ, podium, and splendid kerosene chandelier are all original to the site. Legend surrounds the origin of the chandelier: some tell that it was taken out of a Boston hotel, while others believe that it was a spoil of war from a New Orleans bordello.

A modern, rear addition to the GAR Hall houses the historical society's exhibits and a log cabin, built by John Blomberg in 1868 in Meeker County. The Samstad family purchased the farm and cabin in 1907 and donated the cabin to the society in 1961. The cabin is displayed as a one-room cabin, missing its original sleeping loft, and stocked with early kitchen utensils, a cast-iron stove, a small table with press-back chairs, a wringer washer, and a butter churn.

The Meeker County Historical Society sponsors an ice cream social during the Memorial Day parade, along with other special events throughout the year.

MILLE LACS COUNTY

50. MILLE LACS INDIAN MUSEUM AND TRADING POST
On Highway 169, between Garrison and Onamia.
320-532-3632 or 1-888-727-8386

The new museum interpretive center and restored trading post at the Mille Lacs Indian Museum opened in 1996, replacing an earlier museum building. The museum is located on the southwest shore of Mille Lacs Lake, where the Ayers family originally operated a trading post. The Minnesota Historical Society has operated a museum on this site since 1960.

The new museum's architecture and displays are the result of collaboration between the Minnesota Historical Society and the Mille Lacs Band of Ojibwe. Ojibwe symbolism is embedded in the design, and the central dome is reminiscent of a wigwam. The design for the exterior tile mural is the creation of Batiste Sam, a renowned Ojibwe artist and elder.

The modern museum building offers exhibits dedicated to telling the story of the Mille Lacs Band. Visitors learn about their journey to northern Minnesota, the history of treaties made and broken by the federal government, and the struggle to maintain their culture today. Artifacts from traditional and contemporary Ojibwe culture are also on display. The large Four Seasons Room, a life-size diorama, depicts traditional Ojibwe activities in each season with recreated, traditional Ojibwe dwellings.

In the restored 1930s trading post next to the museum, visitors browse for books, crafts, clothing, and souvenirs. Built in the Craftsman style, the white wood-frame building also features exhibits on the lives of Harry and Jeannette Ayers, who operated this trading post.

Behind the post is the Ayers's house, built in 1941. Not currently open to the public, the house has front and rear gables with a central front door, and a simple peaked overhang tops the entrance. Mr. and Mrs. Ayers's tombstones are located under a tree behind their home.

From the 1920s through the 1940s, the Ayers family also rented tourist cottages along the shore of Mille Lacs Lake. One of the original cottages remains, and visitors can look into the cottage and see a simple stove, table and chairs set, and small bed as it would have looked when rented.

Special events held throughout the year at the site include dance and music events, craft demonstrations and classes, powwows, and other cultural celebrations.

MORRISON COUNTY

51. AXEL BORGSTROM HOUSE MUSEUM

113 Birch Avenue, Upsala, off Highway 238 in Borgstrom Park. 320-573-2335

The Upsala Area Historical Society operates this museum in a 1913 house. Axel and Carrie Borgstrom donated their house and land to display the society's collection of historical artifacts, which included the town's 1928 Reo Speedwagon fire truck. The Borgstrom House Museum first opened to the public in 1984.

Axel, born in 1888, left Sweden with his family in 1893. His father, John S. Borgstrom, helped establish Upsala. Carrie, born in Sweden in 1886, eventually made her way to Upsala, operating a millinery shop for a time. Axel worked at his father's bank, eventually taking over.

In 1913 Carl Hugland, Erick Johnson, and Albert Johnson built the house that the Borgstroms bought in 1914. The house is a modified, one-and-one-half-story bungalow, originally with a hipped roof, large enclosed front porch, two front gabled dormers, and a single side dormer.

The ten-room house offers exhibits on the history of the Upsala area and in particular the Swedish heritage of many early settlers. Many historical items on display in the museum are from the Borgstroms, including a dress Axel's mother wore on the trip across the Atlantic Ocean in 1893.

The main floor of the house has a large kitchen, pantry, formal dining area, sitting room, and bedroom.

The upstairs has more bedrooms and attic storage areas. Over the years the house was expanded and remodeled several times.

The museum holds an annual pioneer work and art day in August.

52. BURTON-ROSENMEIER HOUSE
606 First Street SE, Little Falls, off Highway 27.
320-616-4959

Merchant Barney Burton built this Classical Revival house around 1900. Local attorney and state senator Christian Rosenmeier bought it and eventually passed it on to his son, Gordon. The home was added to the National Register of Historic Places in 1986.

Burton first settled in St. Cloud at age eighteen, where he started a clothing business with his brother. In 1886 he moved to Little Falls where he was active in the business community for more than fifty years. Christian Rosenmeier moved to Little Falls in 1914 with his family to be the city attorney. In 1920 he became vice president of the American National Bank there, and in 1921 he purchased the Burton home before being elected to the

![Burton-Rosenmeier House, Little Falls]

Burton-Rosenmeier House, Little Falls

state senate. Christian's son Gordon, also a lawyer, became the third owner of the house. He fought in World War II and served eight consecutive terms in the state senate. The house is currently owned by the city of Little Falls, which rents the space to the town's convention and visitor's bureau offices.

The home features a large front-entry portico. Above the portico is a balcony edged by a low balustrade. Visitors informally tour the main-floor rooms, including the parlor, dining room, kitchen, pantry, and bathroom. The main floor displays original Rosenmeier family furniture, including a Tudor Revival dining room set with caned chairs and buffet. The house contains all the original woodwork, wood floors, and lighting. The second story has four bedrooms, a porch, and two bathrooms. The bedrooms are furnished with a bedroom set, spinning wheel, cradle, and children's toys. The property also includes a large barn–carriage house.

53. CHARLES A. LINDBERGH JR. BOYHOOD HOME AND INTERPRETIVE CENTER 🎞 🆖
1620 Lindbergh Drive South (Highways 10 and 27), Little Falls. 320-616-5421

This house was built in 1906–07 for Charles A. Lindbergh Sr., a prominent lawyer and US congressman from Little Falls between 1907 until 1917. Lindbergh Sr. had emigrated from Sweden as a child. He married Evangeline Lodge Land in 1901, and they built a three-story mansion at this site that burned down in 1905. After the fire Evangeline wanted a simpler home built, the bungalow that stands here today. The Lindberghs later separated, and their son Charles A. Lindbergh Jr., born in Detroit in 1902, divided his time until 1920 between living here with his mother and visiting his father in his home in Little Falls or Washington, D.C. In 1927, Lindbergh Jr. flew the first solo nonstop transatlantic flight in a plane named the *Spirit of St. Louis*.

Charles A. Lindbergh Jr. Boyhood Home, Little Falls

Visitors see the house as it looked in the period 1917–20. Most of the furnishings and objects in the house belonged to the Lindbergh family and were in the house when they lived there. When Evangeline died in 1954, her possessions were donated to the Minnesota Historical Society. In 1969 the Minnesota Historical Society took over the home, and Charles made visits to the site to tell staff his memories of growing up in the house. He attended the opening of the interpretation center before his death in 1974. The interpretive center includes information about the extended Lindbergh family.

The large, wood-frame bungalow where Charles Jr. grew up was built in 1906–07 over a raised basement formed partly from the foundation of the previous house. His father's business partner, Carl Bolander, designed and supervised construction of the house. The house features an open front porch with steps that lead up the side of the porch.

Visitors enter through the front hall and tour the kitchen, which still contains Evangeline's cookbooks. A doctor's daughter and a teacher, Evangeline first hired a farm wife to teach her how to cook, and she then did the cooking herself. A bathroom features an oak water closet and an enamel sink and tub. Evangeline's bedroom holds an oak dresser, and on top is her celluloid dresser set. The main floor includes a sewing room and a guestroom, used when Evangeline's mother would visit in the summer. Charles Jr. slept year-round on a cot on the porch reached from the dining room (except during storms).

The dining room has a Tudor Revival sideboard, a round oak table with chairs, an oak Morris chair, and a curved glass-front curio cabinet. Wooden paneled doors separate the room from the front parlor, which contains an upright piano, an Empire settee, and bookcases filled with law books. Outside, visitors enter a tuck-under garage. Young Charles kept his ponies here. The car on display is the family's restored 1916 Saxon Six.

The Lindbergh House was placed on the National Register of Historic Places in 1970, and it became a National Historic Landmark in 1976. The home and its surrounding eighteen acres are administered by the Minnesota Historical Society, while the remaining acreage is part of Lindbergh State Park.

54. LINDEN HILL Ⓝ
608 Highland Avenue, Little Falls. 320-616-5500

Two historic homes are located on a nine-acre site overlooking the Mississippi River, now known as the Linden Hill Conference and Retreat Center. Noted Minnesota architect Clarence H. Johnston designed the two houses for Charles A. Weyerhaeuser and Richard "Drew" Musser in 1898 at the height of the Shingle style's architectural popularity. Little Falls contractor A. D. Harrison constructed the dwellings.

The Weyerhaeuser and Musser families operated the Pine Tree Lumber Company in the Little Falls area. Charles, the son of Frederick Weyerhaeuser, married Frances Maud Moon in 1898 in Duluth, and they had two children. Drew, the son of Peter Musser, married Sarah "Sally" Walker in 1903 in Cloquet, and they raised four children. Both families were active philanthropically in the community. In 1908 the Pine Tree Lumber Company donated 3,000 acres of land to the state to become Itasca State Park.

In 1920, when the Weyerhaeusers moved to St. Paul, their home went to the Musser family. Sarah and Drew's daughter, Laura Jane, moved next door into the Weyerhaeuser House in 1956 and lived there until her death in 1989. She suggested the properties be used as a conference and retreat center. The city of Little Falls acquired the deed to the property in 1995 and began work on the Linden Hill Conference and Retreat Center. The homes were added to the National Register of Historic Places in 1985.

The Musser House has exterior white cedar siding with a triangular detail marking the separation from one story to the other. The gables are asymmetrical, in keeping with the Shingle style. The windows are largely grouped in pairs.

The front porch leads to the Great Hall. On the main level are a parlor, music room, dining room, and river porch also used for dining. In the hall, a water fountain shows the Arts-and-Crafts tile work of Ernest Batchelder, a renowned Californian artist. The house has nine bedrooms and eight bathrooms on the second and third (attic) floors. The parlor has elaborate woodwork including an archway that resembles the arches on the front porch, a fireplace nook, and built-in window seats. The music room features original furniture, including a Steel Spenser Orgoblo pipe organ, crystal chandeliers, and a painting by French artist Jean-Baptiste-Camille Corot.

The nearby Weyerhaeuser House is sided with green shingles with the same ribbon of triangular detailing between the floors as the Musser House. There are dormers and two separate front gables. The front face of the house showcases a stained glass window topped with a Gothic arch. The front entrance porch has a separate gabled roof with carved grapevine patterns in the fascia following the roofline. Inside the front porch is a Gothic oak door with arched windows, forged iron crosspieces, and a brass ship doorknocker.

In the Great Hall, living room, and dining room is half-wall paneling. The beamed ceiling in the living room is a fine Tudor detail. A brick fireplace features a carved motto on the mantle.

Laura Jane Musser extensively remodeled the Weyerhaeuser House in the late 1950s and early 1960s, and the décor from this era remains in the lower level. In 1996, the city council and local Musser-Weyerhaeuser Board decided to restore the main floor to its original state.

The grounds contain a small white cottage, a large green barn or carriage house, a tennis court, and a screened-in reception pavilion. English style gardens display statuary and grapevine covered arbors.

The site holds "Christmas in the Mansions" tours each holiday season and other public events.

SHERBURNE COUNTY

55. HERBERT M. FOX HOUSE Ⓝ
10775 Twenty-Seventh Avenue SE, Becker,
off Highway 10. 763-261-4433

The Sherburne County Historical Society, which has a new history center featuring a research library, museum exhibits, and an outdoor interpretive trail, also maintains the Herbert M. Fox House. Samuel Glidden built this small house in 1875, and Herbert Fox purchased the house and eighty acres of land in 1878. He married Ellinor Biggerstaff in 1879, was elected Santiago Township assessor in 1885, and served for a time as a justice of the peace. His son John married Nellie Bartholomew in 1917, and they had two sons. The Fox family lived and farmed the property until 1967, when the US Fish and Wildlife Service purchased the farm to establish the Sherburne National Wildlife Refuge. It was during the house's demolition that workers discovered the unique construction methods on the house and contacted the Minnesota Historical Society for further investigation.

The house was preserved because of its rare vertical-plank construction, which may make it the only remaining house with this type of construction in Minnesota. The house was added to the National Register of Historic Places in 1980. Although the house was moved and subsequent additions removed, the house received National Register status because of its unusual construction techniques. When the Sherburne Historical Society relocated in 2006, the house was moved again. The house now interprets folk construction techniques in Sherburne County.

56. OLIVER H. KELLEY FARM
15788 Kelley Farm Road, southeast of Elk River, on Highway 10. 763-441-6896

This historic farm was the home of the founder of the first national farmer's organization, the National Grange, or Order of the Patrons of Husbandry. Organized in 1867, the Grange, unlike most organizations of that time, allowed women to participate fully in its affairs. The organization's national headquarters were located here between 1868 and 1870.

Oliver H. Kelley Farm, Elk River

Oliver Hudson Kelley, born in Massachusetts, had worked as a telegraph operator in Illinois and Iowa. An introduction to Alexander Ramsey helped him become a messenger in the first session of Minnesota's territorial legislature. In 1852 Kelley married Temperance Baldwin Lane, and together they raised four daughters.

Kelley became a "book farmer" who read and studied the latest innovations in farming. His involvement in the national Bureau of Agriculture led him to start the Grange in 1867 to serve often isolated farmers across the country. He moved his family to Washington, DC, in 1870 and served as executive secretary of the organization until 1878.

Family members owned the farm until 1901. In 1935 the National Grange became involved in restoring the historic house, which was opened to the public for a time in the 1950s. In 1961 the Grange donated the farm and its 189 acres to the Minnesota Historical Society. The house and farm became a National Historic Landmark in 1964 and were added to the National Register of Historic Places in 1966.

Guests start at the visitor center before walking down the path to the farm. The eleven-room wood-frame house has been restored as a typical post–Civil War farmhouse. Oliver H. Kelley built a cabin on this site but did not complete the present home. The root cellar of the house contains the original stone walls from the cabin. Construction of the Italianate-style house began in 1876. It features a front verandah with a central entrance flanked by two large windows.

The side entry would have been used as the everyday entry to the home. A hallway and a staircase lead to the second story. A downstairs bedroom has a spindle bed, Empire secretary, dresser, and rocker. The hallway leads to the kitchen, which contains a sewing machine and wood-fired cook stove. The unfurnished dining room has a bay window.

The front door entrance is reached from a large open verandah. To the left of the main entrance is a large room, arranged as a Grange meeting room. This room has an organ, small desks and chairs, a large bay window, and songbooks from 1874 entitled "Songs from the Grange."

An attached shed at the rear of the house would have been used for drying vegetables and doing laundry. Outbuildings today include a chicken house, machine shed, corn crib, and sheep, calf, and pig pens. The barn was rebuilt in 1974 with portions of the original barn. Today the site is operated as a living-history farm, showcasing agricultural life during the period 1850–70. Costumed guides work the farm doing seasonal tasks using nineteenth-century farm implements, horses, and oxen. Many family-friendly events are held throughout the farming season.

STEARNS COUNTY

57. SINCLAIR LEWIS BOYHOOD HOME Ⓝ
810 Sinclair Lewis Avenue, Sauk Centre, west of Main Street (US Highway 71). 320-352-5201

Renowned writer Sinclair Lewis was born in Sauk Centre in 1885 to Dr. E. J. and Emma Lewis, the third son in the family. Lewis's mother died when he was six, and his father married Isabel Warner a year later. Young Harry Sinclair lived in this house from 1889 until 1903, when he left Sauk Centre to enter Yale University, from which he graduated in 1908. One of his first jobs was as a reporter for a Waterloo, Iowa, newspaper. He began publishing stories regularly in 1915, and six of his twenty-two novels are set wholly or in part in Minnesota. *Main Street* is partially based on his recollections of his hometown of Sauk Centre, which he called "Gopher Prairie" in the novel. Lewis died in Rome, Italy, in 1951, and his ashes were flown to Sauk Centre to be buried with his family in Greenwood Cemetery.

The house museum is operated by the Sinclair Lewis Foundation, which also assists in maintaining the Lewis Birthplace Home and gravesite; it is affiliated with the Stearns County Historical Society. The foundation purchased the house in 1966, which was listed on the National Register of Historic Places in 1968 and became a National Historic Landmark in the same year.

The house has been restored to its late-1880s appearance. The home is in the Upright-and-Wing style, with some Queen Anne decorative elements. The verandah is topped with a small portion of fish-scale detailing and a decorative balustrade with turned finials. Visitors encounter the turn-of-the-century home of Lewis as a young boy, whom friends called "Red." The house is filled with historic memorabilia, and tour guides recount stories of a creative young man whose life was filled with books, mischief, and a thirst for adventure.

The rooms feature wood floors and reproduction wallpapers. The house is furnished with late-Victorian pieces, some of which belonged to the Lewis family. Doctor Lewis's office includes his roll top desk and a radio set given to him by son Sinclair. In the dining room, a clock and the buffet are original to the family. Visitors also may tour the parlor, kitchen, and the second-story bedrooms.

The foundation also operates the Sinclair Lewis Interpretive Center at Interstate 94 and US Highway 71, which offers more artifacts and memorabilia from Lewis's life as an author. Items on display include his college diploma, first editions of books, his writing desk, and his Nobel Prize.

Sinclair Lewis Boyhood Home, Sauk Centre

58. STEARNS COUNTY HISTORICAL SOCIETY

235 Thirty-Third Avenue South, St. Cloud, off Highway 15.
320-253-8424

The nationally accredited Stearns County Historical Society Museum features an extensive research library and modern museum building with a wide range of historical displays, including a hands-on children's area and a replica of a 1930s granite quarry. The grounds of the museum include nature trails and two early log cabins.

The larger of the two is the 1855 log cabin originally built by Balthasar Rosenberger on what is now Sixth Avenue South in St. Cloud. The one-and-one-half-story cabin has a central door with windows on either side. The cabin, which has been used as a home, hotel, fort, jail, courthouse, and claims office, is the oldest remaining home in St. Cloud.

TODD COUNTY

59. CHRISTIE HOUSE HISTORICAL MUSEUM

15 First Street North, Long Prairie, east of Highway 71.
320-732-2514

This 1901 home was built for Dr. George Christie and his wife, Susan. Long Prairie architect C. W. Smith designed and built the home. Eclectic in style, it uses Queen Anne, Classical Revival, and English Arts-and-Crafts elements.

The home's front porch features Ionic columns and capitals, and the roofline has classical cornices with dentil trim. The small foyer door is flanked by two sidelight windows with leaded glass tops. Visitors walk into the library, which has built-in, glass-front oak bookcases. Stained glass windows are seen throughout the house. The dining room has a built-in buffet topped with stained glass windows, and the parlor has a bayed window, also topped with stained glass. Some of the light

Christie House Historical Museum, Long Prairie

fixtures with art glass are from Tiffany & Company. The
foyer features a square newel post topped with a bronze
torchbearer holding an orange swirl of Tiffany glass. The
spindle work and rails, as well as the paneled walls, are
crafted from oak. Wood floors throughout the house
are maple. Several Arts-and-Crafts furnishings belonged
to the family, including a Morris chair with hand-laced
leather cushions. In addition, there is a large collection
of books that belonged to Dr. Christie.

WADENA COUNTY

60. SEBEKA PIONEER PARK
US Highway 71, Sebeka. 218-837-5322

The Sebeka Historical Museum, located in a city park,
is run by the Sebeka branch of the Minnesota Finnish-
American Historical Society. In the center of the park is a
monument honoring area pioneers. Three log buildings
there include an 1887 school, which was the first rural
school in the area, a barn from Red Eye Township, and a
Finnish sauna from New York Mills.

WRIGHT COUNTY

61. COKATO MUSEUM AND GUST AKERLUND STUDIO
175 Fourth Street West (museum) and 390 Broadway Avenue (studio), Cokato, south of Highway 12. 320-286-2427

The building now known as the Gust Akerlund Photography Studio was originally built for photographer Fred Hanson. The one-story wood-frame studio is the only fully restored early photography studio in Minnesota. The Cokato Museum sits behind the studio. Minnesota historical architect Charles Nelson championed preservation of this historic site and wrote the nomination to enter the Akerlund Studio into the National Register of Historic Places in 1977.

August "Gust" Bernard Akerlund, born in Sweden in 1872, settled in Wisconsin in 1894. In 1902 he purchased the photography studio in Cokato, which had been operated by Fred Hanson. In 1906 Gust had the studio moved to its present location and added the posing room with its large skylight to the studio. In 1927, he married Esther Hanson, who was thirty years younger. Gust died in 1954 at age eighty-one, and his wife lived in the studio almost until her death in 1985. Their son, Ted, donated

Cokato Museum and Gust Ackerlund Studio, Cokato

the building and artifacts to the city for restoration, and the studio opened to the public in 1986.

The studio has an impressive posing room with a 10-by-12-foot skylight. The studio's front entrance parlor and powder room are separated from the studio by a dramatic curtain. The formal parlor now serves as a showcase for Akerlund's work, as it would have during his lifetime. A developing room is complete with Akerlund's cameras and developing equipment, and some 14,000 negatives and over 11,000 original glass plates have been saved. His photographs are displayed in the museum.

In the 1930s an apartment was built on the rear of his studio, and these living quarters reflect the décor of the 1930s, when Gust was newly married. All of the furnishings are original to the home. The side porch entrance at the rear of the studio brings visitors past a small bathroom and kitchen. The next room is the family parlor that also served as a bedroom for Ted. The small parlor displays an oak pump organ, a horsehair-covered chair and couch set, and a Mission rocker. The bedroom contains a double-sized metal bed topped with a woven chenille coverlet. A small vanity table, treadle sewing machine, and a steamer chest fill this tiny room.

The Cokato Museum, which has operated since 1976, features a reconstructed and furnished log cabin, a reconstructed portion of round barn, and portion of an original Victorian-era house. A reconstructed Cokato street contains a 1900s hat shop, general store, dentist's office, drug store, tonsorial parlor, and city bank.

62. FINNISH-AMERICAN SOCIETY

10783 County Road 3 SW, Cokato, north of Highway 12.
320-286-2833

The Finnish-American Society of Meeker and Wright Counties maintains a small collection of historic Finnish buildings just outside of the town of Cokato. This area is also known as "Temperance Corner." The 1899

Lee Schoolhouse from French Lake is a clapboard school with a cupola bell tower. The 1896 Temperance Hall sits on its original site. Across the road are an 1856 log cabin and the Savu Sauna, built in 1868.

Annual events at the site include a Memorial Day celebration, a picnic in June, a fall festival in October, and Pikkujoulu (Little Christmas) in December.

63. MINNESOTA PIONEER PARK

725 Pioneer Park Trail, Annandale, on Highway 55.
320-274-8489

Minnesota Pioneer Park is an educational museum with more than twenty structures, dating from 1850 until 1920, that are furnished with period artifacts. Included are an 1850 log house, a 1902 wood-frame house, the 1886 Soo Line depot and caboose, a one-room schoolhouse, and the 1886 Finnish Apostolic Lutheran Church. The pioneer village includes a blacksmith's shop, general store, dentist's office, funeral parlor, jail and print shop, drug store, town hall, millinery shop, harness and buggy shop, post office, and barbershop. The park grounds also include a barn museum and farm machinery exhibits.

The Sorensen family built their log cabin home in Foley in 1884. All the artifacts within the cabin are "hands-on" and may be touched by visitors. A replica sod claim shanty contains furnishings, including a rope bed with a straw mattress and a steamer trunk.

The park hosts a maple syrup festival in April, a chili cook-off in May, a Studebaker day in June, the Immigrants' Christmas celebration in December, and other events throughout the year.

64. WRIGHT COUNTY FAIRGROUNDS VILLAGE

Wright County Fairgrounds, Howard Lake, off Highway 12
and County Road 6. 763-682-7323

The Wright County Historical Society maintains the Collingwood and the Bonk-Leinonen log cabins and a school on the Wright County Fairgrounds in Howard Lake. The 1881 one-room school was moved to the site from Welker.

The Bonk-Leinonen Cabin was built with vertical logs using a rare construction method. The cabin is open during the fair and by appointment.

65. WRIGHT COUNTY HISTORICAL SOCIETY MUSEUM
2001 Highway 25 North, Buffalo, south of Interstate 94.
763-682-7323

The modern Wright County Historical Society Museum in Buffalo includes the Nelsonian, which is a thirty-two-piece one-man-band, and a collection of items that belonged to native son Hubert H. Humphrey, US vice president under President Lyndon Johnson. On the museum grounds are the 1870s Striech-Tuckenhagen-Gritz log cabin and the 1908 Chatham town hall. Both buildings are furnished with historical artifacts and can be toured by request during museum hours.

Wright County Historical Museum, Buffalo

Settlers Square Museum, Warren

NORTHWEST REGION

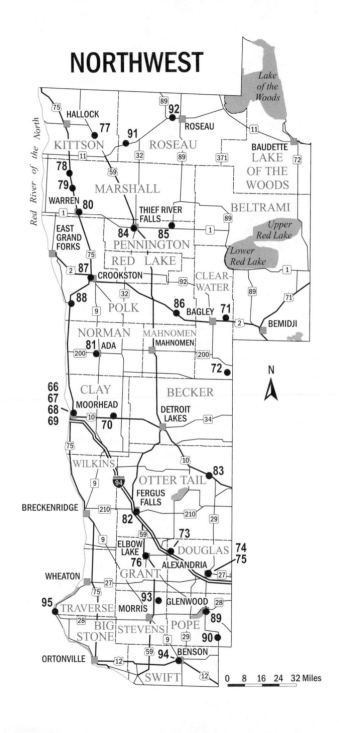

NORTHWEST

Red River of the North

KITTSON
HALLOCK
75
89
92
ROSEAU
91
77
ROSEAU
11
MARSHALL
32
89
371
11
78
59
79
WARREN
80
1
THIEF RIVER
FALLS
84
85
1
89
EAST
GRAND
FORKS
75
PENNINGTON
RED LAKE
87
CROOKSTON
92
88
32
9
POLK
86
BAGLEY
71
NORMAN
MAHNOMEN
MAHNOMEN
81
ADA
200
200
72
66
67
68
69
CLAY
MOORHEAD
BECKER
10
70
DETROIT
LAKES
34
75
WILKINS
83
94
9
OTTER TAIL
FERGUS
FALLS
210
BRECKENRIDGE
210
29
82
73
9
59
74
ELBOW
LAKE
DOUGLAS
75
76
ALEXANDRIA
WHEATON
27
GRANT
27
93
TRAVERSE
GLENWOOD
28
95
MORRIS
89
28
BIG
STONE
STEVENS
POPE
90
ORTONVILLE
12
9
29
94
BENSON
59
SWIFT
12

LAKE OF THE WOODS
Lake of the Woods
11
BAUDETTE
72
LAKE OF THE WOODS
BELTRAMI
Upper Red Lake
Lower Red Lake
CLEARWATER
89
71
1
BEMIDJI
2

N
0 8 16 24 32 Miles

CLAY COUNTY

66. BERGQUIST LOG CABIN Ⓝ
1008 Seventh Street North, Moorhead. 218-299-5520

In 1879 John Gustav Bergquist, an emigrant from Smaland, Sweden, built this log cabin, which is now maintained by the Clay County Historical Society. Bergquist
established the area's first brickyard in 1881 and became
a builder and developer. In 1883 Elijah and Betsy Houck
purchased the cabin, and their farmhand Charles Peterson later bought the farm. In 1977 Charles's son Hank
donated the house and lot to the Bergquist Pioneer
Cabin Society.

The cabin is Moorhead's oldest house still in its original location. A group of volunteers restored the cabin in
1977–81. The cabin was added to the National Register
of Historic Places in 1980 and opened for tours in 1982.
The historical society has operated the cabin since 1991,
displaying local historical artifacts and items from the
Bergquist family. The one-and-a-half-story cabin contains one large open room and a half-story sleeping loft.

The cabin holds an open house in June during
Moorhead's Scandinavian Hjemkomst Days.

67. COMSTOCK HOUSE Ⓜ Ⓝ
506 Eighth Street South, Moorhead, at Fifth Avenue.
218-291-4211

The Solomon G. Comstock home, built in 1882–83, is
an eleven-room, two-and-one-half-story frame house
designed by the Minneapolis architectural firm of Kees
and Fisk. The George Comstock family donated the
house to the Minnesota Historical Society in 1965, and
the dwelling was added to the National Register of Historic Places in 1974. The house is operated by the city of
Moorhead with assistance from the Comstock Historic
House Society.

Comstock House, Moorhead (*Joe Michel/MHS*)

Solomon G. Comstock was a politician and businessman who worked and lived in Moorhead for over sixty years. He moved to Moorhead in 1871 to practice law and later served as a Clay County attorney, a state legislator, and a US congressman. Comstock worked with J. J. Hill to develop the railroad system in the Red River Valley. In 1886 Comstock helped pass a bill to create the state's fourth Normal College in Moorhead, now part of Minnesota State University Moorhead. Solomon Comstock was the college's first resident director, and his son, George, was the second.

The Comstocks encouraged educational opportunities for their children, Ada, Jessie, and George. Ada became the first dean of women at the University of Minnesota and was the first full-time president of Radcliffe College in Massachusetts, serving from 1923 until 1943. The Comstock Halls at Smith College, Radcliffe College, and the University of Minnesota all honor her.

Moorhead's Comstock House, described by architectural historian Roger Kennedy as "Shavian Tory" (based on the work of Victorian English architect R. Norman Shaw), is commonly considered Queen Anne in style.

The home's architectural details include cross timbering, decorative spindles, and gingerbread trim on the front, side, and second-story corner porches.

Inside, double oak doors open onto a hallway filled with custom oak and butternut woodwork. Reproduction wallpaper and hardware is in the Aesthetic Movement–style of the early-twentieth century associated with designer Charles Eastlake, and the hallway displays an Eastlake-style hat rack with a marble top and a calling card desk. The home contains nearly all original furnishings, china, crystal, and decorative objects.

An archway leads to Solomon's law office, which is filled with barrister-style bookcases. One door leads to a sitting room with an Eastlake-style fireplace, and another leads from the hallway to the kitchen and dining room. A butler pantry leads to the kitchen, which has an Estate-brand wood stove.

Visitors take a rear, curved stairway leading to the second story. Ada's room has furniture in the Colonial Revival style of the 1920s and 1930s. Two rooms connect at the front of the house: one was Jessie's, with an Eastlake-style bedroom set and a marble-topped dresser, and the other was the master bedroom, with a cherry-wood bedroom set and a marble-topped washstand.

68. LOG CABIN GALLERY
315 Fourth Street South, Moorhead, off Main Street in Woodlawn Park. 218-299-5252

The Log Cabin Gallery, formerly called the Log Cabin Folk Arts Center, is located in an 1859 cabin built by a group of settlers from Wisconsin. Once part of a cluster of cabins, it survived being burned during the US-Dakota War of 1862. The cabin was used as a stagecoach stop and a land office, moved to a different location, and then occupied until 1930, when the owner donated the cabin to the city.

In 1913 Adolph Bowman donated land to make Moorhead's first city park, Bowman Park. He became the city's first park director and was also involved in the local garden club and historical society. Bowman and his wife adopted the cabin project and restored it for use as the garden club's meeting house. It was moved to Bowman Park, set into the side of a hill, and given a stone foundation and fireplace.

The cabin sits in what is now called Woodlawn Park, owned by the city of Moorhead. An artists cooperative uses the cabin as an art gallery. The 22-by-32-foot building is constructed of oak with a protective exterior façade over the original logs, and it has an open, beamed ceiling over the one large room.

The Log Cabin Folk Arts Center is a participant in the summer River Arts Festival, with an open-air artist market, horse and carriage rides, and outdoor concerts.

69. PROBSTFIELD HOUSE 🔳
County Highway 96, Oakport Township. 701-235-6778

Randolph Michael Probstfield first built a log cabin on his farm in Oakport Township, near what became the city of Moorhead, in 1868–69. Probstfield immigrated to America from Germany in 1852 and was one of the original settlers in Clay County. From 1859 until 1868 he worked for the Hudson Bay Company post at Georgetown. He married Catherine Goodman in 1861, and they had thirteen children.

The family took up residence at the Oakport Farm in 1869. The initial claim of the farm was seventy acres, and by 1880 Probstfield had expanded the farm to 475 acres. Probstfield later served in the state senate from 1891 to 1895. He is known for passing an agricultural bill called the "Drainage Bill" and for his involvement in establishing the state normal school in Moorhead.

Probstfield family descendants owned the farm until 1990, although the farmhouse had fallen into great disrepair. The Minnesota Historical Society included the farmhouse in a 1979 Historic Properties Survey, and the house was added to the National Register of Historic

Places in 1980. The farmhouse today looks like an early 1900s bungalow, due to its wooden siding, gabled roof and bracketed ends, and large front porch. However, the central portion of the house is the original log house. The Probstfield Living History Farm Foundation is currently undertaking the restoration of the home in hopes of opening a house museum at this site.

70. WESTERN MINNESOTA STEAM THRESHERS REUNION
Thresherman's Hill, 25471 Ninetieth Avenue South, Hawley, at County Road 10 and State Highway 32. 218-937-5404

The Western Minnesota Steam Threshers Reunion has been held on Labor Day weekend for more than fifty years. This eighty-acre living-history site comes to life with working historical machines and buildings staffed with volunteers. Vintage buildings include the Rollag general store, a post office, a 1920s Tudor gas station, two schools, a print shop, a sawmill, and three original train depots moved here from the towns of Hitterdahl, Baker, and Hickson.

The Turn-of-the-Century Farmstead includes a red wooden barn and silo built in 1988 to match prototypes of early barns. The red barn is home to draft horses during the reunion, and a new shed and vintage windmill have been added. In 1990 an Upright-and-L farmhouse was built using native rock and local lumber sawed at the site's mill. Salvaged items used in the house include the front door, stairway newell post and railing, and other woodwork. The house is furnished with a spinning wheel, a writing desk, and an early kitchen stove.

The Main Street House is an early-twentieth-century dwelling built by the Fjaer family. In 1986 Bruce Bang donated the house, which was moved to the site. The Italianate farmhouse has a hipped roof with decorative widow's walk, central chimney, and decorative brackets under the eaves. Also on the site are the 1871 Absolum Rushfeldt Log Cabin from Park Township in Clay

County and the 1875 log cabin from Highland Grove Township, which are both open to tours.

During the reunion, volunteers operate a working shingle mill, lumber mill, flour mill, blacksmith shop, and print shop. Activities include tractor pulls, steam plow and thresher demonstrations, daily engine parades, fiddler jamborees, church services, vintage fashion shows, and pioneer craft exhibitions.

CLEARWATER COUNTY

71. CLEARWATER COUNTY HISTORY CENTER
Highway 2 West, Shevlin, west of Shevlin. 218-785-2000

The renovated brick 1911 Shevlin School now houses the Clearwater County History Center, established in 1968. The museum grounds also include the 1880s log schoolhouse that was the first school in the county, the 1936 WPA-built schoolhouse from Vern, and a small 1910 Great Northern Railway depot from Ebro.

The 1904 log cabin, originally located north of Berner in Clearwater County's Greenwood Township, was part of a farm owned by Tober (Claven) Halvorson. The cabin remained in the family until 1954. Donated to the historical society in 1984 and now restored, the cabin is furnished with donated pioneer artifacts.

Clearwater County History Center, Shevlin

72. WEGMANN CABIN AND CCC OLD TIMER'S CABIN
Itasca State Park, Lake Itasca, on US Highway 71.
218-266-2100 or 218-266-36540

Established in 1891, Itasca State Park is Minnesota's oldest state park. In its 32,000 acres are the headwaters of the Mississippi River. In addition to natural attractions, the park features several buildings of architectural interest. Hikers can visit the Wegmann Store Ruins and a replica of Wegmann's original log home. The Civilian Conservation Corps Old Timer's Cabin is located along the Dr. Roberts Trail. It is an original 1930s CCC cabin, staffed by a member of the CCC Association Chapter #93 of Park Rapids during summer weekends.

DOUGLAS COUNTY

73. EVANSVILLE HISTORICAL FOUNDATION
304 Gran Street South, Evansville, off Highway 82.
218-948-2010

The main office of the Evansville Historical Foundation is located in an early 1900s house here. The museum's exhibit hall is in the William L. Beach house, built before 1894. This house displays items donated to the foundation, including pioneer family artifacts, clothing, and items from veterans.

The church house holds area church records and histories and is a study center. The living room is furnished with items from the Reverend S. J. Kronberg, a pioneer pastor at Christina Lake Lutheran Church in rural Evansville. The second-floor bedrooms display items related to the Boy and Girl Scouts, the 4-H Club, and other collections.

The museum grounds also include the brick one-room District 90 schoolhouse, a late-nineteenth-century furnished log cabin, the Eagle Lake Township hall, a church, and a recreated sod dugout. Displays in the township hall include items from the original Evansville post office, businesses, schools, the fire department, and the Evansville Garden Club. An annex added to the hall displays Evansville's first horse-drawn fire engine, a buggy, and other large items.

74. FORT ALEXANDRIA AND RUNESTONE MUSEUM
206 Broadway, Alexandria, north of Third Avenue.
320-763-3160

The Fort Alexandria and Runestone Museum, established in 1958, features exhibits on the history of the Kensington Runestone, the Vikings, Native Americans, early area immigrants, and the founding of Alexandria.

The controversial Kensington Runestone was found in 1898 on Olaf Ohman's farm near Kensington. Runes carved on the stone are said to describe the Vikings being in Minnesota in 1362. The stone's authenticity has been studied and fiercely debated since its discovery.

An assortment of buildings on the museum grounds form a modern reconstruction of Fort Alexandria, built in 1862 by the Minnesota 8th Regular Infantry to provide protection to settlers during the US-Dakota War. The fort was originally located two blocks east of this site. In the original fort, J. H. van Dyke built a log general store and post office. Today the museum contains a replica of this general store that is fully stocked with period items such as stoves, wash bins, wooden and metal tools, and a loom. The museum also includes an 1885 log cabin, an 1883 wash house, a log blacksmith shop, and a Burlington-Northern caboose. The 1885 schoolhouse from Moe Township is reputedly one of the earliest schools in Douglas County. The log church was reconstructed using logs from a building in Carlos Township, and it is similar in style to the original church built at Fort Alexandria. The church features an early pump organ and a pulpit.

A modern building houses the agricultural museum, which contains early tools, carriages, and photographic exhibits. Here is a forty-five-foot reproduction of a Viking merchant ship called the *Snorri*, a three-quarters replica of a ship found submerged in the waters near Roskilde, Denmark. The ship was built by the American Museum of Natural History in consultation with the Viking Ship Museum in Roskilde.

75. KNUTE NELSON HOUSE 🏠
1219 Nokomis Street, Alexandria, south of Twelfth Avenue.
320-762-0382

This 1874 house, which is maintained by the Douglas County Historical Society, was built for Minnesota's first foreign-born governor, Knute Nelson. Born in Norway in 1843, Nelson and his mother immigrated to Chicago when he was six years old. Nelson served in a Wisconsin regiment in the Civil War and studied law at the University of Wisconsin in Madison. He married Nicolina Jacobson, and they had five children. Nelson became an attorney and moved to Alexandria to set up his private practice in 1871. He served as county attorney, district attorney, state legislator, governor, and then twenty-eight years as a US senator. Nelson died in 1923 at age eighty while still in office.

After his daughter Ida died, Nelson's will specified that the house be given to the Norwegian Lutheran Church to be used as a home for elderly men. The house was used in that way for thirty-eight years. Later the historical society moved the house two blocks, but it is still located on Nelson's original property. The house was added to the National Register of Historic Places in 1978, and the historical society restored the house and opened it as a museum in 1987.

Nelson built the first portion of a small farmhouse on his property in 1871. The house is painted white and features a main gabled portion with an L-shaped wing. He added a formal living room and large bedroom to the house in 1900. In 1915 he added a dining room, kitchen, and four bedrooms to the second story.

Knute Nelson House, Alexandria

The small entrance hallway has a replica of Nelson's office on one side, the parlor and dining room on the other. Nelson's office features oak receptacles from the Alexandria post office and an oak desk from the county jail. The museum displays the "K. Nelson Attorney at Law" sign that hung in Nelson's early law office. Across the hall is the family parlor with an Eastlake settee, a marble-inlayed table from Sicily, and chairs from the Nelson family. The dining room contains a built-in buffet that displays the Nelson family's Bavarian china and a dining set with pressback chairs. A main floor bedroom located off the parlor has the Nelsons' original bedroom furniture. Here is Nelson's shaving kit with his personalized razor, hat, trophy cups, and a collection of maps, including a 1902 map of Douglas County. The kitchen and pantry, part of the 1915 addition, contain a Globe-brand stove, Hoosier Cabinet, and wooden ice box.

The second-story bedrooms are set up with displays of local historical artifacts, including a schoolroom, newspaper room, church room, and military room. The lower level contains the society's Family Research Library.

GRANT COUNTY

76. GRANT COUNTY HISTORICAL SOCIETY MUSEUM
115 Second Street NE (Highway 79E), Elbow Lake, east of Highway 59. 218-685-4864

The Grant County Historical Society Museum features displays including fossils of prehistoric creatures, a collection of beaded Native American garments and weapons, a birchbark canoe, a scale model of Fort Pomme de Terre, an ox cart, and an early stagecoach. The grounds hold a furnished pioneer log cabin and a one-room school. The relocated early-twentieth-century school was once the Pleasant View District 7 School.

Ole Halvorson Flor, an immigrant from Trondheim, Norway, built the log cabin in 1865. It has two rooms downstairs and two bedrooms upstairs. The kitchen displays a table and chairs set, washtub, and china hutch. A whitewashed wall separates the kitchen from the parlor, which contains a spinning wheel, pump organ, and other period furnishings.

KITTSON COUNTY

77. KITTSON COUNTY HISTORICAL SOCIETY MUSEUM
322 Main Street East, Lake Bronson. 218-754-4100

Three modern museum buildings have exhibits on the daily life of residents of Kittson County at the turn of the century. Several historical buildings have been moved to the museum grounds, including the Lake

Bronson depot, the Two Rivers Lutheran Church, and the Riverside School from this period.

The paymaster's cottage from the James J. Hill Northcote Farm has also been moved to this site. The farm in Hampden Township was one of Hill's many business enterprises. The small cottage would have been the home and office for the farm's paymaster.

Erick Norland, who settled in the area in 1878, built a log cabin in the late-nineteenth century. This cabin was recently moved to the museum grounds. Norland and his wife, Emma Backman, were reportedly the first Swedish settlers in Kittson County. The small, one-story cabin contains two wooden cots, a treadle sewing machine, a cast-iron stove, and a blanket chest.

MARSHALL COUNTY

78. OLD HOME TOWN MUSEUM
608 Fifth Street, Stephen, off Highway 75.
218-478-2456 or 218-478-2420

In 1990 a group of citizens purchased H. C. "Cutsy" Swanson's 1916 foursquare house to use for the Old Home Town Museum. The Swanson family ran the local newspaper, *The Messenger*, from the 1920s until the 1960s. The house is furnished with donated items and collections.

Behind the house a modern building is filled with early farm implements, tools, and other equipment, including a replica stagecoach, a chapel, items from Nyland's Shoe and Leather shop, which operated from 1895 through 1999, and a large doll collection. Visitors can also learn about Michael McCullough, known as Tamarac Mac, who was a founder of the town in 1878.

The museum holds an ice cream social and a Summerfest each year.

79. OLD MILL STATE PARK CABIN
33489 Two-Hundred-and-Fortieth Avenue NW, Argyle.
1-800-652-9747 or 218-437-8174

Inside the boundaries of Old Mill State Park are the
Larson Gristmill and a pioneer log cabin. The original
Larson family cabin was destroyed, and the current
cabin was donated in 1973 by Lloyd Setterholm, whose
property adjoined the park.

In 1882 Lars Larson homesteaded here. His son
John started a mill at a different location. In 1897 two
mills were moved to where the "old mill" now stands.
The state bought the mills in 1937. The original 1880s
gristmill is powered today by a Case 359 steam engine,
rebuilt in 1958.

During park hours, the cabin can be viewed through
the gated doorway. The grounds also contain a two-hole
outhouse, a split-rail fence, and a well. In August, visitors
can buy flour milled in the Old Mill.

80. SETTLERS SQUARE MUSEUM
808 East Johnson Avenue, Warren, Marshall County
Fairgrounds. 218-745-4803

The Marshall County Historical Society established the
Settlers Square Museum in 1979. The Village Square con-

Old Mill State Park, Argyle

tains façade storefronts along a boardwalk, including a post office, bank, law office, drug store, saloon, general store, hotel, millinery, barbershop, and the Berget Studio.

Historical buildings moved to the site include the 1880 Warren Soo Line railroad depot, the late-nineteenth-century Cook School, and the 1893 Alma Lutheran Church. The 1886 log cabin was built by Medore Landreville and his wife, who traveled to the area from Canada by an oxen-pulled wagon. The cabin, moved here from Bloomer Township, had stayed in the family until the museum acquired and restored it. The cabin has a kitchen and a parlor divided by a short wall and a sleeping loft, and it is furnished with items from the late-nineteenth and early-twentieth century.

The museum has a unique "cook car," a portable field kitchen used to feed threshers, that may be the only one on display in the entire state. The wooden structure has a stove, table, benches, cupboard, and shelves. The main museum building houses machinery, tools, and other historic artifacts, including a replica Red River ox cart that retraced a pioneer trip from Pembina, North Dakota, to St. Paul, Minnesota in 1958.

NORMAN COUNTY

81. PRAIRIE VILLAGE
104 First Street East, Ada, on Highway 200.
218-784-4989 or 218-784-4141

The Norman County Historical Society operates a county historical museum and a nearby prairie village. The Prairie Village contains buildings moved to the site from throughout the county, including the 1884 Nordby rural school, the 1891 Pontoppidan Church, the 1888 Bethany Church, a log house, a store, a depot, the Bank of Ada, the Gray Graphic newspaper office, and a barbershop with original flooring, cabinets, chairs, and early hair cutting equipment.

The Prairie Village also contains a large modern building filled with antique machinery and a modern log museum building filled with displays of historical artifacts. The Norman County Genealogy Society has their collections and meeting space in the new log building.

OTTER TAIL COUNTY

82. CARLSON LOG CABIN
1110 Lincoln West, Fergus Falls. 218-736-6038

The Otter Tail County Historical Society Museum features rotating exhibits, a gift shop, and the E. T. Barnard Research Library. Permanent exhibits include the reconstructed Carlson Log Cabin, which is furnished with period artifacts. The museum also features a log outbuilding that is furnished as a trapper's shanty.

83. FINN CREEK OPEN AIR MUSEUM
55442 Three-Hundred-and-Fortieth Street, New York Mills, off Highway 106. 218-385-2233

The New York Mills–Finnish American Society has preserved this Finnish homestead as an open-air museum. In the early-twentieth century Siffert and Wilhelmiina Tapio and their family settled on this farm. It is located near Finn Creek, named in honor of the many early Finnish settlers in this area. The museum was organized in 1976 when the society bought eighteen acres from the second owner, Arnold Tumberg.

The farmstead contains the original 1900 home, log barns, and sauna. The white, wood-frame farmhouse contains items from Finnish settlers. A red barn, log well house, and corncrib are also on the property. The 1890 Oak Knoll country school and the Ottertail town hall were moved to this site, and a chapel and general store were built here.

Annual Finnish festivals include craft sales, enter-

Finn Creek Open Air Museum, New York Mills

tainment, and Finnish foods and refreshments. Activities include an antique tractor pull and a sawmill and threshing machine demonstration. The farm holds a summer folk festival and Talvi Juhla, a Finnish winter celebration.

PENNINGTON COUNTY

84. PEDER ENGELSTAD PIONEER VILLAGE
825 Oakland Park Road, Thief River Falls,
off Highway 32 South. 218-681-5767

The Pennington County Historical Society operates the Peder Englestad Pioneer Village. The society, which dates to 1938, dedicated the pioneer village in 1976. This village recreates the history of Pennington County through nineteen historic buildings.

The village includes the modern Englestad Museum, six log cabins, a blacksmith shop, barbershop, general store, the one-room Little Oak Schoolhouse, the Asphult Church, and an exhibit building with agricultural machinery and antique cars. The two-story wood-frame Viking Soo Line railroad depot was used for freight and passenger service. The one-story brick Great Northern depot was used mostly for freight service.

The Queen Anne-style Hamre House is a two-and-one-half-story home with a Dutch gambrel front-gabled roof. The house features a receded entrance supported by one column. The front bay window and side extensions are typical of the Queen Anne style.

Peder Engelstad Pioneer Village, Thief River Falls

The village's log cabins include the Olson Cabin, Swanson-Bray Cabin, Berg Cabin, Muzzy Cabin, Noper Cabin, and Homestead Cabin. All feature different construction techniques, served differing purposes, and were moved here from around the county.

85. GOODRIDGE AREA HISTORICAL SOCIETY

Pennington Street East and Urdahl Avenue West, Goodridge.
Historical society president, 218-378-4380

The historic buildings preserved and renovated by the Goodridge Area Historical Society, formed in 1977, are located around the downtown area. The town was built in 1914–15, when it became the terminus of the Minnesota Northwestern Electric Railway.

The buildings include a country store museum, a log cabin and log barn built with vertical logs, the Northwestern Telephone Building, and a two-story house dating to 1914. The Goodridge depot, also called the Northwestern Electric Railway depot, is located on Urdahl Avenue West, and the Woodrow School Museum is across from the depot. The modern Settler's Center is also available for tours.

POLK COUNTY

86. LEWIS WILLIAM LARSON HOUSE
Melland Park, Highway 2 East and Sather Drive, Fosston.
218-435-1959 or 218-435-1313

The house built in 1887 by Lewis William Larson and now known as the East Polk Heritage Center was one of the first wood-frame houses in Fosston. In 1886, when the Great Northern Railroad was building the line between Crookston and Fosston, Larson, his brother, and another partner started a general store in Fosston. His business interests expanded to include a flour mill, sawmill, lumber mill, and real estate. He also built the Fosston Opera House, operated the Rosebud Stock Farm, and started the first co-op creamery in town. Larson served two years as the mayor of Fosston.

The Larson house stayed in the family until 1976, when it was converted it into a board and care home that preserved as much of the home's original character as possible. In 1986 Allen Potvin donated the house to the East Polk Historical Society, and it was moved to its current location. The exterior of the house is simple, marking it as typical of the Upright-and-Wing design. The small corner front porch, which has its own separate roof, extends from the front of the side gabled wing.

The door from the front porch leads to the front hall and the main floor living area. The parlor contains

Lewis William Larson House, Fosston

the piano originally used in the Fosston Opera House. The dining room contains an oak dining room table set with pressback chairs and a glass-front oak china hutch. The kitchen features a Hoosier cabinet and an Estate-brand cast-iron stove. The second story has the original bedrooms used by the Larson children. One room is filled with early dolls and toys, one is displayed as a schoolroom, and one is a doctor's office. The bathroom has its original claw foot bathtub, the first one of its kind in a Fosston home.

Other structures on the property include a small cabin built by local legend Peder LeDang, otherwise known as "Cordwood Pete." The small cabin, made of slim vertical logs mortared together, has many of LeDang's simple furnishings. Steve and Joe Rapisarda of Ebro built another cabin on the property in 1994–95 that is furnished with early artifacts but is mostly used for arts and crafts demonstrations and displays.

Special events include a Christmas festival, arts and crafts demonstration days, and children's tours.

87. POLK COUNTY HISTORICAL SOCIETY MUSEUM
719 Robert Street East, Crookston, on Highway 2 East.
218-281-1038

The museum contains exhibits on Polk County history and a complete genealogical research center. The three modern Polk County Historical Society Museum build-ings are named Millenium, Centennial, and Agriculture. Exhibits include a kitchen, bedroom, and parlor from a pioneer house. A recreated main street includes a gen-eral store, dentist and doctor's offices, and a barber and beauty shop.

An 1876 log house and an 1892 wood-frame house are located on the museum grounds. The one-and-one-half-story log cabin has one large open room that is sim-ply furnished. A separate wood-frame summer kitchen sits next to the cabin. Other buildings on the grounds include a blacksmith shop and the District 226 rural school. The museum has a large Red River ox cart on display on the grounds.

88. SAND HILL SETTLEMENT
415 Riverside Drive, Climax, north of Highway 220.
218-857-2241

The Sand Hill Settlement Historical Society was established in 2000 to create a working pioneer farmstead. Scandinavian immigrants settled the area in the late-nineteenth century, and it is still primarily an agriculture-based community. The society's main goal has been re-creating a historic farmstead park along the Sand Hill River. The park will eventually include a house, log barn, windmill, and other buildings.

The 120-year-old log Estenson family barn, originally sited about three miles north of the park, was taken down in 2002, rebuilt using new local logs, and given a new cedar shake roof. One of the earliest cabins in this part of the Red River Valley, originally built and used by the Estenson family, was recently moved back to the Minnesota side of the Red River. The cabin is now on a foundation at the farmstead restoration site.

The society hosts a summer festival in July, and will add events when the restoration of the site is complete.

POPE COUNTY

89. POPE COUNTY HISTORICAL SOCIETY
809 Lakeshore Drive South, Glenwood, off Highway 104.
320-634-3293

The Pope County Historical Society in Glenwood has a modern museum displaying recreations of a fur-trapper's cabin, dress shop, doctor's office, barbershop, general store, post office, telephone office, and a parlor, bedroom, and kitchen that would have been a typical at the turn-of-the-century.

On the museum grounds are six historical buildings that were moved to the museum site. These include the furnished Pleasant Hill Schoolhouse, St. Paul's Episcopal Church, a furnished lake cabin, and the Torguson Log Home, furnished with pioneer artifacts. Another log cabin on the grounds was originally built by Ole Peterson in Gilchrist Township. Peterson was one of the organizers of Pope County, and his cabin served as the first Pope County courthouse.

90. TERRACE MILL DISTRICT 🔳
27165 Old Mill Pond Road, Terrace, south of Glenwood on Highway 104. 320-278-3728

William Moses and brothers John and George Wheeler built the first mill on this site in 1870. In 1895 the mill was dismantled and moved to Brooten, and in 1903 J. M. Danials built the current flour mill. The flour mill was operated by three different owners until 1948. In 1967 the mill site was abandoned, and in 1979 the Terrace Mill Foundation purchased the mill and adjoining

Terrace Mill District Heritage Cottage, Terrace

property. The Terrace Mill District was added to the National Register of Historic Places in 1979.

The district includes the 1903 flour mill, 1903 stone arch bridge, 1882 dam on the Chippewa River, a 1930s fieldstone house belonging to the miller, a late-nineteenth-century log cabin, and the Heritage Cottage. A former general store located near the site now is operated as a café. The town of Terrace also contains a historic school used as the township hall and the Chippewa Falls Church.

A log cabin was moved to the site and restored in the early 1980s. The Scandinavian cabin was one of the first homes in Terrace. It features pegged oak logs and corner notches and is furnished with pioneer-era items. The Heritage Cottage, built in the 1950s, is decorated with typical Scandinavian furnishings and folk art items. The Norwegian-style painted furniture includes a double bunk bed, table, cupboard, and other small pieces.

The mill features historical displays on the history of the mill and the Terrace arts community. One portion of the mill is used as an art gallery with rotating exhibits.

The Terrace Mill Foundation sponsors musical and theater events, art shows, and art classes. Special events include Summerfest in June, an Irish festival in August, and a fall festival and fiddler's contest in September.

ROSEAU COUNTY

91. PELAN PIONEER PARK
Highway 11, Greenbush, between Karlstad and Greenbush.
218-782-2417

The Pelan Pioneer Park is a collection of restored buildings highlighted with wildflower gardens. The Karlstad depot, church, school, log blacksmith shop, white wood-frame store, and log cabin are located on this site.

The late-nineteenth-century cabin is a one-story building made of squared logs, with whitewashed interior walls. Simple period furnishings include a table and chairs set, a metal twin bed, a hutch, and a washstand.

92. PIONEER FARM AND VILLAGE
Highway 11 West, Roseau. 218-463-3052

The Pioneer Farm and Village focuses on the history of agriculture and pioneer life in the Roseau area. The museum includes a pioneer settler's log cabin, a trapper's cabin, and an early barn. The Nannestad Lutheran Church and the 1894 log cabin Pine Creek church, the first organized church in the county, were also moved to this site.

The 1905 Halvorson Cabin has an enclosed stairway to the sleeping rooms upstairs. A log interior wall separates the kitchen from the family parlor. The kitchen features an enameled stove, a pie safe with punched tin doors, and a table and chairs set.

A boardwalk connects the recreated village buildings. These include L. B. Hartz's General Store, the Casperson rural school, the Jorgenson blacksmith shop, a print shop, the Ross post office, the Nannestad Fellow-

Pioneer Farm and Village, Roseau

ship Hall, the Bruss cigar shop, and a dentist's office. The modern Holm and Bjorkman Exhibit Hall has displays of farm equipment, tractors, and threshing machines.

The site hosts a pioneer farm festival in August.

STEVENS COUNTY

93. TRANTOW LOG CABIN
Scandia Wetlands Environmental Lab, Framnas Township.
320-589-1719

The Stevens County Historical Society is located in 1905 Carnegie library built by F. A. Hancock and designed by the Minneapolis architects Sedgewick and Saxton. (It was listed on the National Register of Historic Places in 1983.)

The historical society also maintains a log cabin, which was dismantled and moved to the Scandia Lab site in 1994. German immigrants Adolph and Auguste Trantow built this cabin in 1871–72. It features German-style log construction with dovetailed corners. Because the most common form of immigrant dwelling here was probably the sod dugout—Stevens County was mostly a treeless prairie in the 1870s—the Trantows had to haul their logs from Pomme de Terre Lake, several miles from the cabin's original building site. This cabin is believed to be the only surviving log house of the few originally built in Stevens County.

SWIFT COUNTY

94. RINDAHL LOG CABIN
2135 Minnesota Avenue (West Highway 12), Benson.
320-843-4467

The modern Swift County Historical Museum features a log cabin built by Fredrik Rindahl in 1873–75 in Six Mile

Grove Township. In 1980 the Hanson family donated the log cabin to the Swift County Historical Society. The cabin was installed in the museum in 1981, and it has been restored to its original appearance. Period furnishings in the cabin include a small table, bed, baby cradle, and potbelly stove. The cabin originally had a sleeping loft, which was removed to fit the cabin into the museum.

TRAVERSE COUNTY

95. SAM BROWN MUSEUM Ⓝℝ
Sam Brown Memorial Park, Browns Valley.
320-695-2312 or 320-695-2110

In 1863 this log cabin was built on Kettle Lake near Fort Wadsworth (today Fort Sisseton). In 1866 the fort closed, and in 1871 Major Joseph R. Brown bought the cabin and moved it to Browns Valley. The cabin was added to the National Register of Historic Places in 1986 as the Fort Wadsworth Agency and Scout Headquarters.

Major Joseph Brown served as the military agent at the Upper and Lower Sioux agencies from 1858 until 1861. During the US-Dakota War of 1862, Brown rejoined the army and fought in battles at Birch Coulee and Wood Lake. He then served as a special agent and commander of scouts at the Fort Wadsworth Agency near the Minnesota-Dakota border. His family moved to Browns Valley and lived in this cabin. After 1871 his son, Samuel Jerome Brown, and family lived in the home. The cabin was used as the first post office, with Sam Brown serving as the first postmaster. This cabin also served as a trading post, stagecoach stop, and a haven for travelers and the sick.

The cabin is named for Samuel Brown, "Paul Revere of the Frontier," who in 1866 rode 120 miles through a snowstorm to warn settlers of a Dakota attack, which turned out to be false. Caught in the snowstorm, Sam required a wheelchair for the rest of his life.

The large, one-and-one-half-story cabin features a door on the left side of the front gabled end of the cabin. It has a window on its front face, two windows in the gabled end of the sleeping loft, and side windows on the first and second floors. The cabin displays the 1870 piano that Major Joseph Brown had shipped from New York by rail to Willmar and brought to Browns Valley via ox cart. Sam Brown's wheelchair is also on display, as well as many other local historical artifacts.

The Browns Valley Historical Society also owns and maintains the 1892 St. Luke's Episcopal Church. This wood-frame church was the first church in Browns Valley. It has all the original interior woodwork, including the original altar and kneeling bench.

Forest History Center, Grand Rapids

NORTHEAST REGION

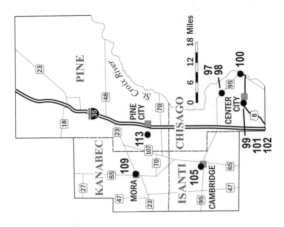

NORTHEAST

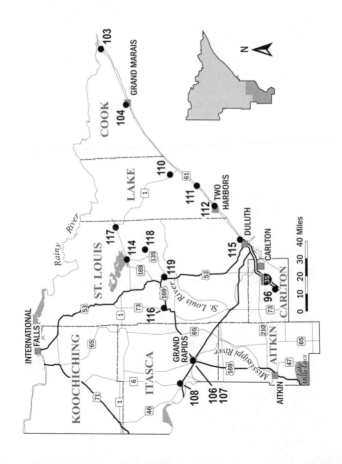

CARLTON COUNTY

96. CARLTON COUNTY FAIRGROUNDS
Carlton County Fairgrounds, Barnum, on County Road 6 (Front Street). 218-879-1938

The Carlton County Fairgrounds contains a small village of historical buildings. Among the original structures moved here are a log cabin, log barn, church, and school. The log cabin is furnished with early-twentieth-century items such as a cook stove, desk, table and chairs, cradle, and bed. An original 1940s state forest ranger's cabin is also located at this site. Recreated buildings include a post office, general store, and blacksmith shop.

The Carlton County History and Heritage Center is located in the 1920 former Cloquet Public Library, which was added to the National Register of Historic Places in 1985. The Renaissance Revival–style brick library was designed by Kelly and Shefchik.

CHISAGO COUNTY

97. ALMELUND THRESHING SHOW
State Highway 95, Almelund. 651-583-2083

The Almelund Threshing Company operates the historic buildings at this site. The 1876 Chisago County courthouse was moved here in 1990 from Main Street in Center City (thus removing the building from the National Register of Historic Places). This large white building stands high above the other structures and helps visitors locate the property from the road. A pioneer log cabin is currently being restored. The Clover Blossom School was once used as the Shafer Township Hall. A re-created Amador Mercantile and Uncle Dan's Blacksmith Shop are open during the Threshing Show.

On the second weekend in August, the grounds become the site of the Almelund Threshing Show. Activities include tractor pulls, vintage car and truck shows, live music, a flea market, and a petting zoo. Popular events include demonstrations of blacksmithing, glass blowing, and other early trades. Volunteers operate the sawing, shingle, and lathe mills during this weekend only.

98. AMADOR HERITAGE CENTER

Maple Lane, Almelund, near County Highway 12
and State Highway 95. 651-269-3580

The Friends of the Amador Heritage Center, a branch of the Chisago County Historical Society, operate this site. The museum is located in a 1910 two-room brick school-house in Almelund.

In addition, the seventeen-acre site has a log gra-nary, an 1865 Swedish log cabin, and a small 1840–50s log cabin. Another log cabin dating from the 1890s was recently reconstructed.

The society hosts an Apple Festival in September featuring craft demonstrations and Model-T and wagon rides.

99. CHISAGO COUNTY HISTORICAL SOCIETY

13100 Third Avenue North, Lindstrom, at Olinda Trail.
651-257-5310

The Chisago County Historical Society's offices, meeting rooms, exhibits, and research library are housed in an early-twentieth-century house in residential Lindstrom. The house was moved from downtown Lindstrom after it was donated in 1996.

The house is in the Upright-and-Wing style, with the receded wing allowing for the creation of an L-shaped front porch. The porch features a separate roof and turned porch supports. The front gable end of the main house has a plate glass picture window and Queen Anne decorative fish-scale details beneath the roofline.

The Chisago County Historical Society has long been active in preserving historical structures throughout the county, including other houses in Lindstrom, Amelund, and Chisago City. Most recently the Society has been restoring the 1920s Arts-and-Crafts foursquare home of the Moody family in Chisago Lake Township for use as a house museum. The 1915 Moody Family round barn was added to the National Register of Historic Places in 1980.

100. W. H. C. FOLSOM HOUSE MUSEUM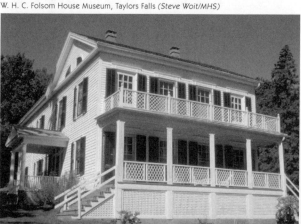
272 Government Street West, Taylors Falls,
north of US Highway 8. 651-465-3125

The 1855 William Henry Carman Folsom House is situated in the bluff-side settlement above Taylors Falls known as Angel Hill, which overlooks the St. Croix River. The settlement's Greek Revival-style homes are white clapboard, and many feature green shutters. The wood-frame Folsom House reflects the New England heritage of Folsom, a pioneer lumberman who arrived in Minnesota from Maine. The house has a New England–style Greek Revival façade, but there is also French influence in the two-tiered galleries that Folsom added along the east face. The Folsoms' grandson moved into the home in the 1930s and added plumbing and electricity. The State of Minnesota purchased the property in 1968 for use as a Minnesota Historical

W. H. C. Folsom House Museum, Taylors Falls *(Steve Woit/MHS)*

Society museum site, and the W. H. C. Folsom House Museum opened in 1970 for tours. In 1978 the Taylors Falls Historical Society began offering guided tours of the site, and in 2005, a gazebo matching the original was recreated on the museum grounds to celebrate the home's 150th anniversary.

W. H. C. Folsom, who first arrived in Stillwater in 1845, settled in Taylors Falls five years later. After working as an independent logger, he helped form the St. Croix Boom Company and became a mercantile owner, postmaster, and civic developer. Folsom served as a state representative for one term and state senator for six terms. He helped write the state constitution.

Visitors to his home enter on the south side through a side vestibule. A wide staircase to the second story is located across from the entryway. On the east side of the home, forming the front façade of the house, are the double parlors, separated by pocket doors. The rooms were cleverly built to save money on taxes, which were levied on basis of the number of windows and rooms in the house.

One parlor was used as a sitting room, the other as a music room. The 1848 rosewood piano was shipped by riverboat from Boston. The indent in the pine floor beneath the damper pedals is evidence of the instrument's frequent use. A small office holds Folsom's book collection and many leather bound ledgers from his store. In the dining room a clever walnut table, set with Tea Leaf–pattern family dishes, has leaves that self-store underneath. All the items on display belonged to the Folsoms.

A wide staircase leads to the second story. Three of the five original bedrooms are on view. The nursery is filled with children's toys and a unique potty chair. The bedrooms above the front parlor have pocket doors identical to those below. Glazed French doors lead to the second-story porch. Artifacts in these bedrooms include turn-of-the-century razors, eyeglasses in their original cases, a wedding dress, a Civil War uniform and canteen, and other items of family clothing.

Each year the museum's rooms are decorated in a different theme for the Christmas festival, which is held the first two weekends after Thanksgiving.

101. GUSTAF'S HISTORIC HOUSE MUSEUM [NR]
13045 Lake Boulevard (Highway 8), Lindstrom.
651-257-5310

In 1879 Gustaf and Helena Anderson built this brick Italianate home, now located on the main street in Lindstrom and managed by Chisago County Historical Society. It stands out among the simple wood-frame structures commonly built by the area's Scandinavian immigrants.

Anderson immigrated to Michigan from Sweden in 1864, where he worked in the copper mines near Lake Superior. In 1867 he moved to Minnesota and then to Montana to pursue a successful venture in gold speculation. When he returned to Minnesota, he purchased farms for his family in the Franconia area of Chisago County and built this house in town for his retirement home. Five generations of the Anderson family lived in the house. The house was used for a time as a collectibles shop before being restored by the historical society. The house was added to the National Register of Historic Places in 1980.

The brick home features wooden decorative trim in keeping with the Italianate style and a wooden front porch and balcony along the front face of the house with carved spindles in the balustrade. Along the east side of the house is a double bay window.

The home's front door opens to the vestibule containing the staircase to the second story. A large formal parlor in the front of the house contains an Eastlake rocker, a large display case with historical items, and Swedish woven wall hangings. The parlor opens onto a formal dining room, furnished with a formal dining room set. This room connects to a large kitchen and meeting room, which has a farmhouse-style kitchen table.

102. KARL OSKAR HOUSE

Kichi-Saga Park, Lindstrom, off County Road 25.
651-257-2519, 651-257-5855, or 651-257-1177

The Karl Oskar House was moved to Kichi-Saga Park, just south of Lindstrom, in 1995 through the efforts of the Lindstrom Historical Society and other organizations. King Carl Gustaf XVI and Queen Silvia of Sweden visited this site with much fanfare in 1996.

Swedish author Vilhelm Moberg used this house as a fictional model in his popular novels about Swedish pioneers in the Chisago Lakes area after he visited the town for research and inspiration. This is the house he envisioned his characters Karl Oskar Nilsson and Kristina building for their final years.

Many Swedish immigrants to this area came from the Smaland region of Sweden. The Carl and Lena Kajsa Linn family constructed this farmhouse in the 1860s. In 1995 owners Gerald and Urban Holt donated the house to the historical society. The house originally sat about a mile from the park but now rests on a hill overlooking South Center Lake.

The one-and-one-half-story farmhouse was in great disrepair when it was acquired, and much of the exte-

Karl Oskar House, Lindstrom

rior has been replaced. The fish-scale decorative trim at the roof's peak is original. The interior of the house still retains much of its original character. The walls, ceiling, and flooring of the rooms are tamarack, cedar, and pine wood. The kitchen floor has wide-width boards that were hand-hewn by the builders.

Visitors enter onto a small porch, which has one door to the summer kitchen and another door to the family parlor. The kitchen contains a Favorite-brand cast-iron stove made in Piqua, Ohio, and the parlor features a Singer sewing machine. The daybed and drop-leaf table are original to the Linn family who first built the house. Located off of this room are two small bed-rooms with furnishings and items from area Swedish-immigrant families, including a restored spinning wheel made in Sweden, an immigrant chest, and the Linn family's cradle. A steep, narrow set of stairs leads from the kitchen to the upper floor. This open attic, which con-tains the Linn family loom, would have been a sleeping room during the summer months for the children of the family or farmhands.

The barn was moved to this site in 2003 from Scan-dia and is used as a tool shed. The museum is located near many sites and landmarks connected to the area's Swedish immigrants, including the nearby Glader Ceme-tery, the oldest Swedish pioneer cemetery in Minnesota.

COOK COUNTY

103. GRAND PORTAGE NATIONAL MONUMENT
211 Mile Creek Road, Grand Portage, off US Highway 61.
218-387-2788

Grand Portage National Monument is a partial recon-struction of the North West Company's busy fur trading headquarters sited on the western shore of Lake Superior from 1778 to 1802. The North West Company, headed by Simon McTavish in Montreal, created one of the largest and most profitable fur trading companies in North America. Canoes full of furs were carried more than eight miles from inland Fort Charlotte to Grand Portage Bay on Lake Superior. This spot became the site of the annual summer Rendezvous, where voyageurs from Canada, Minnesota, and Wisconsin would meet to exchange fur pelts for goods and, possibly, money.

Today's rebuilt structures represent what were the business quarters of the post. They were rebuilt in the 1970s by the National Park Service, which operates Grand Portage National Monument, established here in 1960. The architectural style of the buildings reflects the French-Canadian heritage of the voyageurs and influences of the area's Ojibwe Indians. The log construction style is *Poteaux sur sole* (post-on-sill), sometimes called Canadian Frame. The buildings were constructed of hand-hewn, squared cedar and white spruce logs with cedar and pine shingles.

Historical records show that in 1793 the palisade contained sixteen buildings, with several more buildings

Grand Portage National Monument, Grand Portage *(National Park Service)*

outside. Inside the palisade today are a reconstructed
gatehouse, lookout tower, Great Hall, and kitchen. The
reconstructed buildings are furnished with replica and
authentic artifacts. A reconstructed canoe warehouse
and dock sit outside the palisade. To the west is a recreated Ojibwe village with birchbark structures: summer and winter wigwams, work shelters, and a long
house. Southwest of the stockade is a voyageur encampment that would have housed as many as 1,200 men
during the Rendezvous.

The first excavations and reconstructions at Grand
Portage were done in 1936–38 by the Minnesota Historical Society with the help of Grand Portage Ojibwe tribal
members. The palisade and several other buildings have
since undergone further reconstruction. Excavation of
the kitchen site in the 1970s uncovered nearly 15,000
artifacts. Items such as dish and bottle fragments, tools,
and nails are on display. Each summer, costumed interpreters recreate life in the encampment and Ojibwe
village circa 1797.

104. LIGHTKEEPER'S HOUSE MUSEUM Ⓝⓡ
8 Broadway South, Grand Marais. 218-387-2314

The Cook County Historical Society Museum is located
in an 1896 wood-frame lightkeeper's house. This building served as a home until the mid-1920s, when the
North Superior Lifeboat Station was built and this house
became the commander's home. The keeper's house,
which was added to the National Register of Historic
Places in 1978, is filled with donated furnishings and
local historical artifacts.

The Cook County Historical Society maintains
other historic buildings. The 1896 Church of St. Francis
Xavier, an Indian mission church, is one mile east of
Grand Marais at Chippewa City. Built by Jesuits in 1896,
the church served the Catholic community until 1936
and was added to the National Register of Historic Places
in 1986.

Edblad Cabin, Cambridge

The 1907 Jim Scott Fishhouse in Grand Marais was listed on the National Register in 1986. A 1930s replica of a fish house holds the society's fishing exhibit. On the same site is the thirty-five-foot fishing tug, *Neegee*, built in the mid-1930s in Grand Marais by the Scott family. The Scott family tug served as the workhorse of the harbor until the mid-1960s.

The recreated Johnson Heritage Post in Grand Marais, built on the site of Charlie Johnson's 1904 trading post, has ongoing exhibits of the art of the North and a permanent collection from Anna Johnson.

ISANTI COUNTY

105. EDBLAD CABIN AND WEST RIVERSIDE SCHOOL [N]
Polk Street NE (County Road 14) and Three-Hundred-and-Thirty-Ninth Avenue NE, Cambridge, north of Highway 95.
763-689-4229

The West Riverside Historic Site, which includes the 1859 Edblad Pioneer Log Home and the 1900 West Riverside School, is operated by the Isanti County Historical Society. Issac and Christine Edblad were Swedish immigrants who moved to the banks of the Rum River in 1859. They built a two-room cabin, which became a home for travelers and an early site for church services. In 1864 the Cambridge Lutheran Church was first organized in the Edblad cabin.

In 1972 members of the Edblad family bought the Youngquist cabin, which was similar to their ancestor's home, and had the cabin moved to the museum site. The restored cabin contains a kitchen, parlor, and sleeping loft furnished with some original Edblad family items as well as other period artifacts. Furnishings include a cast-iron cook stove, a zinc-topped dry sink, a desk used in the O. P. Edblad Store from the 1860s, and an iron bed.

The one-room brick West Riverside School built in 1900 was added to the National Register of Historic Places in 1980. A bell tower projects above the front entrance. The exterior features patterned brickwork, a set of four windows on each side, and a rear chimney. Beginning in 1902, Cambridge Lutheran Church members taught immigrant children the Swedish language here during the summer months.

The Isanti County Historical Society, which has operated the site as a museum since 1971, holds summer camps and a Swedish language and culture camp in August.

The Isanti County Historical Society Resource Center also has a log cabin next to its modern museum building on the county fairgrounds. This 1870s cabin that was moved to the site in 2004 is being restored.

ITASCA COUNTY

106. FOREST HISTORY CENTER 🏚
2609 County Road 76, Grand Rapids. 218-327-4482

The Forest History Center consists of log buildings in a recreated logging camp, as well as a visitor's center with extensive exhibits. The logging camp appears as it would have during the winter of 1900, when it might have housed eighty men. Winter camps were usually built to last one season while the immediate area was logged; new camps would have been built each season for harvesting new stands of timber.

This large site was originally home to three different farms. The Blandin Paper Company donated the land to the Minnesota Historical Society in the 1970s for the creation of a museum to preserve and interpret the area's logging history.

The log buildings here include a dining structure, an office, a blacksmith shop, a saw-filer's shack, an outhouse, a root house, and a horse barn. A log cook shack is outfitted with two working cast-iron stoves. In the log office, lumberjacks could purchase tobacco, clothes, boots, medicines, and other necessities visible on the shelves. A sleep camp has bunks on both side of the building with a stove and clothes drying racks in the middle of the room.

A recreated 1934 Minnesota Forest Service patrolman's cabin also at the site features a bunk, desk and chair, small stove, and enamelware items. In addition, visitors may climb the nearby original one-hundred-foot-tall fire tower for spectacular views of the area forests, or hike down to the Mississippi River banks and climb aboard the 1901 river wanigan, which served as the floating cook shack during river log drives. Costumed living-history interpreters demonstrate camp life in the early-twentieth century.

107. JUDY GARLAND MUSEUM
2727 US Highway 169 South, Grand Rapids.
218-327-9276 or 1-800-664-JUDY

The Judy Garland Museum is the restored childhood home of film and stage star Judy Garland. The house has been restored to the way it looked in the mid-1920s when her family lived in Grand Rapids.

Judy Garland Museum, Grand Rapids

Frances Ethel Gumm (Judy Garland) was born on June 10, 1922, in Grand Rapids. She lived in Grand Rapids for four and a half years. Judy's father, Frank Gumm, sang tenor, performed, and managed theatres. Judy's mother, Ethel Marion Milne, played piano at the movie theatre in Grand Rapids. "Baby Gumm" gave her first public stage performance at age two in her father's New Grand Theater. She and her two older sisters performed throughout northeast and north central Minnesota before moving to California in 1926. The sisters performed as the "Garland Sisters" in Chicago during the 1934 World's Fair. Judy Garland signed a movie contract with MGM at age thirteen in 1935.

Judy Garland, best known for her role as Dorothy in *The Wizard of Oz,* made thirty feature films. She starred in her own television shows, gave theater and nightclub performances, and recorded more than twenty-four albums. She died in London in 1969.

The simple wood-frame farmhouse in Grand Rapids was built by Andrew and Mary Shook in 1892 and was first moved from its original site in the summer of 1938. In 1994, two acres of land was donated to the Judy

Garland Museum, and the house was moved again to its current location. Restoration of the house was completed in 1996.

Visitors enter through the rear of the house via the new museum. The fully furnished main floor rooms include the kitchen, dining room, and front parlor, which contains a Lester grand piano similar to one that would have been played by Mrs. Gumm. The second story housed the two family bedrooms and bath. The older sisters' bedroom has two beds, early clothes, and a bureau. The parents' bedroom, which baby Frances shared, has an iron bed and dresser. The room is decorated with family photos and 1920s jewelry, hats, and period clothing.

The complex features two museums: a Judy Garland Museum with the largest collection of her memorabilia in the world and a Children's Discovery Museum. New York City interior designer Marc Charbonnet collected and donated nearly 100 period artifacts for furnishing the house, and his Judy Garland memorabilia collection has been loaned to and exhibited in the museum.

Garland's birthday is celebrated on June 10 with a festival.

108. WHITE OAK FUR POST
33155 Highway 6, Deer River. 218-246-9393

The White Oak Fur Post is the re-creation of the original 1798 North West Company post built on the Mississippi River several miles from the current site. This post was a winter quarters that included a smokehouse, log living structures for the voyageurs, clerks, and director, and a company store. The recreated Ojibwe village is located in the woods near the fur post. The Great Hall and Learning Center houses the Rick Balen Library, the White Oak Society Office, and a dining hall.

The site hosts the White Oak Rendezvous and Festival in August, a dog sled race and New Year's celebration in January, a Mother's Day dinner in May, and a variety of other events that often feature costumed interpreters.

KANABEC COUNTY

109. KANABEC HISTORY CENTER
805 West Forest Avenue, Mora. 320-679-1665

The Kanabec County History Center Museum features exhibits on the history of the area, including the strong presence of Swedish immigrants. The museum's research facility is available for local history and genealogical research.

Outside the modern museum buildings are the re-located Whittier and Coin schools, a Great Northern Railroad caboose, gardens, a collection of vintage farm implements, and an early fire engine. Between the two schools is a historic log cabin, furnished to show how a pioneer schoolteacher would have lived.

LAKE COUNTY

110. FINLAND MINNESOTA HERITAGE SITE
5653 Little Marais Road (County Road 6), Finland, off Highway 61. 218-353-7380

The Finland Minnesota Heritage Site, located on the John Pine Homestead, features an interpretive center and original log buildings crafted in the Finnish style. Finnish and other Scandinavian immigrants first settled here in 1895. The area became the town of Finland in 1907, when logging railroads were built. By 1935 there were about 180 Finnish families in the 500-acre area working in farming, logging, and taconite mining.

A log home is furnished with items from the early-twentieth century. The one-and-one-half-story log house features a right-side door with two front windows and a central chimney stack. The log sauna was moved to the site. A farm implement display and an heirloom veg-etable garden showcase the farming techniques of early settlers. An open-air stage area is used for music festivals and other events throughout the year.

111. SPLIT ROCK LIGHTHOUSE 🏛 ®

3713 Split Rock Lighthouse Road, Two Harbors.
218-226-6372

This historic site includes the original brick Split Rock Lighthouse, a fog-signal building, the lighthouse keepers' homes, and the ruins of a tramway to the lake. The lighthouse, built in 1910, served ships until 1969, the year the Split Rock Lighthouse site was listed on the National Register of Historic Places.

In 1907, after several disastrous storms, Congress appropriated $75,000 for building a lighthouse and fog signal on a 130-foot cliff above Lake Superior's hazardous coastline. Split Rock Light Station was completed by the US Lighthouse Service in 1910. The service operated the lighthouse to protect iron-ore shipping until 1939, when the US Coast Guard took command. The station closed when modern navigational equipment had made many lighthouses obsolete. Visitors can now take a self-guided tour at their own pace or a 45-minute guided tour. Tours focus on the lighthouse itself, which visitors can enter and explore, and one of the three lighthouse keeper's houses.

The State of Minnesota obtained the landmark in 1971, and the Minnesota Historical Society has operated the historic site since 1976. The buildings have been restored to their appearance before 1924, when the lighthouse usually was reached by water. In 1980 the historic site area was expanded to twenty-five acres, and the head keeper's dwelling was restored. A visitor center has exhibits and a video orientation.

The lighthouse site includes three brick foursquare houses that housed the lighthouse keepers and their families. Behind the houses are two of three original storage barns that were converted to garages after the site could be reached by road.

Entering the head keeper's house, visitors pass through the hall into the kitchen, which displays a Favorite-brand cast-iron stove and a porcelain sink where water was pumped from Lake Superior. A narrow pantry opens onto the dining room, which is furnished with an Arts-and-Crafts–style oak table and chairs and a desk with a captain's chair. Visitors then enter the front parlor with its daybed, Singer sewing machine, library table, Edison canister music machine, and an oak rocker. From the hallway visitors may climb the staircase to the second floor. Upstairs are three furnished bedrooms and a bathroom, which contains a typical wooden water closet with a porcelain stool and an oak water chamber.

Special events include a November ceremony to mark the sinking of the famed freighter *Edmund Fitzgerald*. Family activities are held throughout the museum's open season.

112. TWO HARBORS LIGHTHOUSE [NR]
520 South Avenue, Two Harbors, south of Highway 61.
218-834-4898

In 1884 the first shipment of iron ore left Agate Bay on Lake Superior. Construction of the Two Harbors Lighthouse to protect ships and their cargo occurred in 1891–92. After many years of service, Congress transferred ownership in 1999 from the US Coast Guard to the Lake County Historical Society. The society then completed a major restoration effort involving fundraising, grant writing, and a public awareness campaign.

The Two Harbors Lighthouse, which was added to the National Register of Historic Places in 1984, features castle-like details including graduated brick embellishments around the top and along the two edges of its lower front façade. The attached brick lighthouse keeper's house has a front gable end and a side gable portion next to the tower.

Today the lighthouse serves multiple purposes. Fully rehabilitated by the historical society, it is still a working lighthouse. Three bedrooms are rented as bed-and-breakfast rooms to recreate the lighthouse keeper's experience, and the revenue generated helps fund restoration and maintenance of the lighthouse. The main floor has a kitchen, pantry, dining room and living room. The second floor has bedrooms and a bathroom. Furnishings throughout the house are from the early-twentieth century. The Lake County

Two Harbors Lighthouse, Two Harbors

Historical Society also operates the Depot Museum and the 3M Museum in Two Harbors.

Other original buildings on the grounds include the oil house, storage building, fog-signal building, skiff house, and the 1894 wood-frame assistant keeper's house.

PINE COUNTY

113. NORTH WEST COMPANY FUR POST

12551 Voyageur Lane, Pine City, off Interstate 35.
320-629-6356 or 1-888-727-8386

The North West Company, a fur trading company based in Montreal, Quebec, employed more than one thousand men in 1805. This log outpost on the Snake River was one of many in a whole system of posts designed to move furs from the interior of North America to Montreal. John Sayer, a wintering partner in the company, ran this post on the Snake River. Sayer and his company of eight voyageurs, one clerk, and his family came to this place on October 1, 1804, and stayed only one winter. The company abandoned the post on April 27, 1805, returning to Grand Portage in the spring to deliver their shipment of furs and collect their pay.

In 1963 the Minnesota Historical Society began excavating the site. Sayer's journal of his year at the post was used for reconstructing and interpreting the site. The recreated post opened to the public in 1970. Today the modern visitor's center is located west of Pine City amid farm fields. Once visitors leave the center and take the path through the forest to a ridge overlooking the Snake River, they are transported to the year 1804, when most inhabitants of the area were Ojibwe. Visitors at the site enter a small Ojibwe encampment. The recreated birchbark home is lined with furs and blankets and has a fire pit in the center. Small groups may go inside and sit on the blankets and learn the traditions of the Ojibwe.

A path leads on to the reconstructed post. The original structures were built in six weeks in the fall of 1804 by Sayer's workers. Pine logs created a stockade, and a log row house is the only building inside the post. Four doors along one side lead to separate chambers. One would have housed five voyageurs in 1804. In this room are two bunks, a corner fireplace, a small table, samples

North West Company Fur Post, Pine City (*Joe Michel/MHS*)

of voyageur clothing, and games the men would have played to pass the time. The next section of the row house is the clerk's quarters, and beyond those were Sayer's quarters, with a large bed, a trundle bed for children, a fireplace, a table set with dishes, and children's toys and games.

The last room in the row house is the trade shop. It exhibits samples of different types of animal pelts, as well as a counter and shelves lined with trade goods including blankets, cloth, beads, string, muskets, and powder.

The site holds many special events including a North West Company Rendezvous and War of 1812 event.

ST. LOUIS COUNTY

114. BOIS FORT HERITAGE CENTER AND CULTURAL MUSEUM
1500 Bois Forte Road, Tower, off Highway 169.
218-753-6017

The Bois Fort Band of Chippewa developed this heritage center and cultural museum on their reservation. The museum, called the Atisokanigamig, or Legend House, opened in 2001 on the shores of Lake Vermilion at Fortune Bay Resort Casino.

The museum features a painted mural that tells the story of the Ojibwe migration to northern Minnesota. Exhibits detail traditional activities such as fishing, harvesting wild rice, and collecting maple syrup. In addition, the museum offers information on how fur trading, logging, and mining impacted the area and the life of the band members. A recreated birch bark canoe made at the Nett Lake Reservation is on display, as is a traditional dwelling crafted from cedar and birch bark. The grounds also include an authentic tipi.

115. GLENSHEEN, CONGDON ESTATE
3300 London Road, Duluth. 218-726-8910 or
1-888-454-GLEN

Noted architect Clarence H. Johnston designed Glensheen Mansion between 1905 and 1908 for the family of Chester A. and Clara Bannister Congdon. The five-story mansion has thirty-nine rooms including fifteen bedrooms, fifteen fireplaces, ten bathrooms, a grand reception room, a library, a parlor, a dining room, a glass-enclosed breakfast room, and custom-designed furniture. The grounds include seven acres of manicured landscapes, with formal gardens, a carriage house with a carriage collection on view, a gardener's cottage, boathouse, clay tennis court, pier for yachts, marble fountain, and stables. The Jacobean Revival–style manor resembles an early-seventeenth-century English country estate. The brick house features carved stone parapets with stone pediments around windows and doorways, and the front façade has three parapeted gables with third-story balconies.

Glensheen, Duluth

Chester A. Congdon was an attorney who arrived in Duluth in the 1890s and grew wealthy during the iron ore boom. He met Clara Bannister while attending Syracuse University in New York, and they married in 1881. He later made his fortune in land speculation and mining in northern Minnesota and Arizona. The couple had seven children and also raised a nephew in their mansion home.

In 1968, Congden heirs gave Glensheen to the University of Minnesota to preserve the mansion and use it for "public pursuits." In 1979 the estate opened as a museum. The estate was added to the National Register of Historic Places in 1991. The University of Minnesota Duluth operates the house museum.

Glensheen's large main hall is located off the front entrance, which connects to the long hall to the east and entrances to the kitchen, servants' room, dining room, and breakfast rooms. The hall to the west leads to the reception room, den, living room, and library. Highlights of these rooms include reproduction sixteenth-century furniture, custom art-glass, silk damask wall coverings, ceilings accented with gold leaf, distressed cypress woodwork, an Algerian marble fireplace, and a mahogany Steinway grand piano.

From the hallway visitors ascend the staircase, accented by a stained glass window made by the Linden Art Glass Company in Chicago. Visitors can view Marjorie's bedroom, which is furnished in the Georgian style. The master bedroom features Art Nouveau sconces with Quezal art-glass shades and walnut Arts-and-Crafts–style furniture. The remaining bedrooms have color themes—red, pink, gold, and gray—and distinctive original furniture. The hallway also leads to the three simple servant bedrooms, and a back servant staircase goes to the servants' dining room on the main floor, two pantries, and a large open kitchen.

The first-floor butler's pantry has one door to the dining room and one stained glass door to the breakfast solarium room. The solarium, designed by Minneapolis's John Bradstreet, is an Arts-and-Crafts masterpiece, with oak-leaf-and-acorn–patterned stained glass, a ceiling light fixture from the Minneapolis Handicraft Guild, a built-in fountain, and Rookwood tiles. A door from the solarium leads to the dining room. Georgian-style furnishings in this room include a mahogany dining room table and chairs set, two side boards, a buffet, and two china cupboards. From the main hallway a rear formal staircase leads to the walk-out lower level. Here is a billiard room with a 1908 oak billiards table.

Glensheen holds a variety of special tours and events throughout the year and may be rented for private events.

116. IRONWORLD DISCOVERY CENTER
801 Highway 169 SW, Chisholm. 218-254-7959
or 1-800-372-6437

Ironworld Discovery Center, located on the edge of the Glen Pillsbury mine, collects, preserves, and interprets the history of Minnesota's Iron Ranges. The campus includes a museum and archives, a park and railroad, living-history sites with historic buildings, and two stage venues.

Ironworld Park and the Glen mining "location" (company town) feature numerous historic and recreated exhibit buildings and living-history interpretive sites. Furnished structures include the Civilian Conservation Corps History Center Museum, a northwoods cabin, a Native American camp, a Sami camp, and a

Ironworld Discovery Center, Chisholm

Norwegian *stabbur* (storage house). The 1904 homestead features a cabin built by Herman Thompson in Bear River, a log barn, and a sauna.

Visitors can ride a 1928 vintage trolley two-and-a-half miles to Glen, a former mining community that was active between 1903 and 1935. The site includes a 1905 Finnish boarding house, a 1908 location house, 1915 Wilpen depot and railroad bunkhouse, and numerous displays of vintage mining equipment.

The site features costumed interpreters, educational programs, and an annual Polkafest in June.

117. DOROTHY MOLTER MUSEUM

2002 East Sheridan Street, Ely, on Highway 169.
218-365-4451

On this museum site are two original cabins from Dorothy Molter's Isle of Pines resort on Knife Lake. Molter, a local legend, was the last legal resident of the Boundary Waters Wilderness Area. Called the "Root Beer Lady" and the "Nightingale of the Boundary Waters," she welcomed thousands of visitors who arrived by canoe at her island home each year, where she was known for her homemade root beer, nursing skills, and harmonious way of living with nature. She left her home in 1986 after spending over fifty years living on the island.

Bill Berglund built the cabins out of vertical, thin logs in the 1920s when he operated the Isle of Pines resort. In 1934 Dorothy moved to the island to help Berglund run the resort, and when he died in 1948, he left the resort to Dorothy.

The museum in Ely opened in 1993 as a memorial to Dorothy. The two cabins are called the Winter Cabin and the Point Cabin. The Point Cabin was one of the four rental cabins at the resort. Molter's original broken canoe-paddle fence and rock garden have been rebuilt around the cabins. From the wash stand set up outside as her "powder room" to the root beer-making equipment, visitors can see how Dorothy lived her unique life.

118. SISU HERITAGE HOMESTEAD TOURS ⓃⓇ
Highway 135 and Highway 21, Embarrass. 218-984-2084

Heritage Homestead Tours offers caravan-style guided driving tours to Finnish pioneer homesteads, a craft shop, and other stops. Many of these authentic homesteads, including houses, saunas, and barns, were added to the National Register of Historic Places in 1990. The restoration of these buildings and the installation of historical information signs were a part of the federal Take Pride in America Program.

The sites included on the tour are the 1910–15 Gregorius and Mary Hanka Homestead, the 1900 Mike and Mary Matson Farmstead, the 1930s Erick and Kristiana Nelimark Sauna, the Sisu Tori Museum and Craft Shop, the information center, and the 1887–1948 Pyhala Homestead. Buildings are crafted of logs in the Finnish style, with the exception of one block house on the Pyhala homestead. Four log buildings are completely restored on the Pyhala farm, and restoration is in the progress on the Hanka Homestead.

119. VIRGINIA HERITAGE MUSEUM
800 Olcott Park, Virginia, at Ninth Avenue North.
218-741-1136

Virginia Heritage Museum consists of an early-twentieth-century house formerly occupied by the park superintendent, a 1910 log house, and a 1930s tourist cabin. The buildings contain both permanent and changing exhibits focusing on the area's cultural and industrial development, including the lumber industry.

Olcott Park, opened to the public in 1910, was named after W. J. Olcott, an officer of the Great Northern Mining Company. The 1916 stone entrances to Olcott Park remain standing today. In 1935, the Civil Work Administration planted more than a thousand trees in the park and constructed Monkey Island, which operated from 1941 until 1964.

The Work Projects Administration also constructed a three-acre rock garden in the park in the 1930s. The park had a famous illuminated fountain built by the General Electric Company in 1937, one of only a few built in the United States. The greenhouse has displays of exotic flowers and is a favorite city landmark.

The 1910s house, now home to the museum, was the park superintendent's home. The house was moved from a nearby location to its present site in 1915, when a second story was added. In 1917 and 1940, further improvements were made to the house. The original staircase with wooden newell posts and the fireplace remain distinctive features in the house.

A 1910 log house is located adjacent to the main museum building. The two-room, one-and-one-half-story cabin was built in 1910 by Finnish homesteader Oscar Holkko. The furnished cabin includes kitchen utensils, a dresser, baby carriage, phonograph, 1912 washer, rotary sewing machine, china cupboard, and early tools.

The 1930s tourist cabin was also moved to this site. This is a typical rental cabin that was built and operated by the city of Virginia. The cabin now exhibits early dentist equipment and barber and beauty shop artifacts that include an early permanent wave machine.

John Lind House, New Ulm

SOUTHWEST REGION

SOUTHWEST

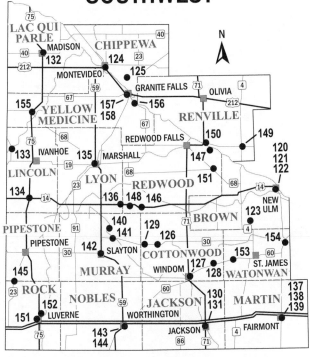

LAC QUI PARLE

MADISON
132

CHIPPEWA
124
125

MONTEVIDEO

GRANITE FALLS
156

OLIVIA

RENVILLE

YELLOW MEDICINE
155
157
158

REDWOOD FALLS
150
149
120
121
122

IVANHOE
133
135

MARSHALL

LYON
136 148 146

REDWOOD
147
151

LINCOLN
134

PIPESTONE
145

PIPESTONE

140
141

142
SLAYTON

129
126

MURRAY

COTTONWOOD
127
128

BROWN
123
NEW ULM

154
153
ST. JAMES
WATONWAN

ROCK
152
151
LUVERNE

NOBLES

WINDOM
130
131

JACKSON

WORTHINGTON

JACKSON

MARTIN
137
138
139

FAIRMONT

143
144

0   6   12   18   24 Miles

BROWN COUNTY

120. WANDA GÁG HOUSE
226 Washington Street North, New Ulm, off Highway 14.
507-359-2632

This 1894 Queen Anne–style home was built for Anton Gág and his family. It is now named for his daughter, Wanda Hazel Gág, a children's-book author and illustrator. Her many works include *Millions of Cats*, published in 1928, which won the prestigious Newbery Award. In 1988 the Wanda Gág House Association purchased this house to create a museum honoring the artistic accomplishments of Wanda, her father Anton, and her sister Flavia.

Bohemian-immigrant Anton Gág operated a pho-

Wanda Gág House, New Ulm

tography studio and later partnered with decorators Chris Heller and Alexander Schwendiger. They are known for their work throughout Minnesota, including the mural paintings and other decorative works in the Holy Trinity Cathedral and Turner Hall in New Ulm.

Wanda was the eldest of seven children born to Anton and Elizabeth Gág. Each inherited a love for the arts. When both parents died, the children sold their home in New Ulm, and Wanda moved her siblings to Minneapolis to live with her in 1918.

The exterior of this family house has an open-turret balcony, two-story double bay windows, decorative bands of fish-scale trim, spindlework with gingerbread brackets, and upper roof finials. This lively exterior ornamentation and the wood plank siding have been repainted with the seven original colors chosen by Anton. There are seven different window shapes and seven rooms in the house. Visitors can tour the family bedrooms and the attic.

Visitors enter the front hall to the parlor, where the borders painted by Anton Gág have been restored. In the connecting dining room is a collection of lithographs of Wanda's illustrations. From the front hall, visitors take the staircase to the second floor. At the top of the stairs is Anton's *malzimmer* room, or painting studio. This room has large windows and an alcove with a skylight. Anton later moved his studio to the attic when the growing family needed another bedroom.

The house celebrates Wanda's birthday in March and holds events to honor local and regional authors throughout the year. At Christmas, trees throughout the house are decorated according to themes from her books.

121. FRIEDRICH W. KIESLING HOUSE [NR]

220 North Minnesota Street, New Ulm, near Third Street North. 507-233-2268

The 1861 Friedrich W. Kiesling House is the oldest frame building in New Ulm remaining in its original location.

In recent years, the house has been the home of the Council of the Arts in New Ulm.

This two-and-a-half-story wood-frame house is Greek Revival in style. An important defense post during the US-Dakota War of 1862, the house was at one point filled with hay so that it could have been burned to create a diversion if New Ulm were attacked. The house, a private residence until 1970, was listed on the National Register of Historic Places in 1972.

The house's main floor contains wide, wood plank flooring and a central staircase to the second floor. The lower level has an exhibit gallery featuring monthly showings by artists.

122. JOHN LIND HOUSE ℝ
622 Center Street, New Ulm, at State Street. 507-354-8802

Designed by Frank Thayer, the John Lind House was built in 1887. John and Alice Shepard Lind and their four children resided in the house from 1887 until 1901. The house was later sold and converted to a duplex, and in 1974 it was added to the National Register of Historic Places for its political and architectural significance. The Lind House Association opened this house to the public in 1984.

John Lind was the first Swedish-born American elected to the US Congress. He served four terms. A Spanish-American War veteran and diplomatic representative to Mexico under President Wilson, he was also Minnesota's fourteenth governor. Elected in 1899, he served for two years. He then practiced law in Minneapolis until his death in 1930.

This brick and stone Queen Anne–style house features a distinctive round bay tower. The front porch curves around the rounded tower alcove on the first story. The restored woodwork has been painted with the home's original colors of maroon, green, and black. Decorative porch supports, cornices, and wooden fish-scale shingles are all distinctive details of the Queen Anne style.

During the initial restoration, a carpenter recreated the parlor's original stairway and pocket doors, which had been removed. The dining room fireplace was found hidden behind plaster and restored. The house still retained some original wood trim and moldings. One stained glass window in the parlor was intact, and others in the dining room and stairway hall were recreated. The wallpaper throughout the house matches the style seen in early photographs of the rooms.

The front foyer leads into a large parlor that features a rosewood spinet and built-in bookcases topping built-in benches in a bay window nook. The dining room contains the original fireplace and is furnished with a 1920s Colonial Revival oak dining set. At the top of the second-story staircase, a wide, open hallway is used as a sitting area. The former bedrooms are now used as offices and are not available for touring.

During the Christmas season, the Lind house is decorated in the Victorian style and is open for tours and special teas.

123. OMSRUD-THORDSON-TORGRIMSON LOG CABIN
Lake Hanska County Park, Brown County. 507-439-6313 or 507-233-6640

The Omsrud-Thordson-Torgrimson Log Cabin located in Lake Hanska County Park in Brown County was built in 1857–58 by Thord Omsrud, Torgrim Torgrimson, and his wife Kari Omsrud. They emigrated from Valdres, Norway, to Wisconsin in 1852 and were the first Norwegians to arrive in the Lake Hanska area in 1857. The families later changed their name to Thordson.

In 1986 the cabin was moved from Omsrud Lake to its current location. The restored cabin is made out of oak logs and was lived in until 1953. Today the two-story cabin features an open front porch and a decorative gabled window. Items found during a Minnesota Historical Society archaeological dig are on display in the cabin, which is fully furnished with a table and chairs, parlor stove, dishes and linens, rocking chairs, and bed sets.

CHIPPEWA COUNTY

124. HISTORIC CHIPPEWA CITY
151 Pioneer Drive, Montevideo, at US Highway 7 and State Highway 59. 320-269-7636

Historic Chippewa City, a pioneer living-history village, began operations in 1965. Almost two dozen buildings have been moved to or built on site to form this recreated village, which represents a typical pioneer village with wooden sidewalks centered around a village square.

Buildings include the millinery and dress shop, print shop, general store, harness shop, blacksmith shop, law office, fire department, buggy shop, and original Brown Brothers Fuel and Ice building. Historic structures include the 1911 Lund-Hendrickson School and the 1882 Norwegian Lutheran Church. The Chippewa Bank is located in the former Erickson School and features the front door and vault originally from the Eliason Bank in Montevideo. Another building was once a barbershop built by J. M. Severins in 1873.

The museum also features five historic houses. The log cabin used now as the village post office was built in 1870 by Hans Lund and also functioned as the original Reeser post office, which served the Watson area. The log cabin used now as the Burn fur trading post came from Yellow Medicine County and was built in 1871 by Martinus Myhre.

Roloff O. Moe built the Ness House in 1885–86. The main floor includes the living room, two small bedrooms, a kitchen, and a pantry. The kitchen is equipped with a Monarch-brand range and vintage furnishings.

Heinrich Gippe, who was one of Chippewa County's earliest settlers, built his cabin in 1867. The structure displays some of the Gippe family collections. The 1870 cabin built by Bardinus Anderson also served as the first location of Saron Lutheran Congregation.

The museum holds periodic special events and often features costumed interpreters.

125. OLOF SWENSSON FARM

Six miles east of Montevideo on Highway 7 and five miles south on County Road 6. 320-269-7636

The Swensson Farm Museum features the large brick home built in 1901–03 by Olof Swensson and his daughter Katerine. It is now operated by the Chippewa County Historical Society.

The wood-frame house is faced with a brick veneer and set on a foundation of huge local granite stones, hand-cut and laid by Swensson and his daughter. The twenty-two room house sits on a seventeen-acre farmstead with a large timber-framed barn, remnants of a gristmill, and the family burial plot.

Olof Swensson, born on May 19, 1843, in Ostmarken, Norway, married Ingeborg Agnetta Pearson in 1869, and

Olof Swensson Farm, Montevideo

they immigrated to America in 1872. Known for his strong Lutheran beliefs, Swensson created a chapel in his home and held weekly religious services there. He was well-known in the area and ran unsuccessfully for governor of Minnesota.

After Swensson's death in 1923, the farmstead gradually fell into disrepair. In 1967, the property was given to the Chippewa County Historical Society, and in 1974 the house and barn were added to the National Register of Historic Places. In 2003 the historical society completed a $300,000 structural preservation project on the 1880s timber-framed barn.

Visitors are able to tour the home's main floor including the parlor, dining room, library, two bedrooms, kitchen, and two former bedrooms used as utility rooms. Upstairs is a chapel and four rooms. In the basement are several large workrooms, including a woodworking area and metal crafting area.

All of the furnishings in the home are original to the Swensson family, and Olof handcrafted many items in the home, including painting and staining the woodwork. Etched glass graces several doorways, and there is stained glass in the dining room. Visitors to the museum can also view the barn, remnants of the gristmill, the family cemetery, and the Moehring building, which displays vintage farm equipment.

The farm hosts an annual threshing show.

COTTONWOOD COUNTY

126. NELS HYSTAD CABIN
United States Avenue (County 5) and America Street, Storden, north of Highway 30. 507-445-3102

Nels Hystad built this log cabin in 1866 near what became the village of Sunburg. Hystad was a carpenter and a Norwegian immigrant from the island of Stord, for which Storden is named. The cabin was built of white oak trees from Monson Lake.

Nels's grandson, Gerhard Hystad, donated the cabin to the city of Sunburg, where it was displayed from 1955 until 1995. In 1995 citizens of Sunburg donated the cabin to the citizens of Storden. The one-room cabin has a sleeping loft and an added front porch. An 1863 cast-iron stove, baby crib, enamel wash stand, and wooden hutch filled with early kitchen utensils are among the historic items on display.

127. MONSON-CHESTER LOG CABIN
Island Park, Windom. 507-831-1134

Originally located in Jackson County's Christiana Township, this 1869 cabin was built by Mons O. Monson and Thomas Chester on the line between the men's land claims so that they could share the cabin while claiming their homesteading rights. The cabin was later moved to the Monson property and enlarged with an addition that has since been removed. The Monsons raised seven children in the cabin before moving to South Dakota in 1883. Other owners of the cabin included the Julius B. Severson family and Peter Larson.

The cabin was donated to the city of Windom in 1939 and relocated later to its current location. The Cottonwood County Historical Society now cares for the cabin.

128. MOUNTAIN LAKE HERITAGE VILLAGE
County Road 1, Mountain Lake, off Highway 60.
507-427-2023

Mountain Lake Heritage Village contains several historical structures that have been moved to the museum grounds. These include the 1890 Mountain Lake depot and caboose, the Delft post office, the 1903 Odin–Mountain Lake State Bank, and the 1902 Jaeger General

Store, which was moved from Darfur in 1973. Other buildings on the museum grounds include a barber and beauty shop, schoolhouse, blacksmith shop, granary, modern machine shed, hospital, and furniture store.

The museum was built on the land of an 1884 Mennonite homestead. The original Victorian-style farmhouse has an attached red barn and detached summer kitchen. Some historic artifacts remaining from these early Russian immigrants include *kistes* (steamer trunks), clocks, butter churns, and a cradle. The Minnesota Telephone Museum and Prairie Interpretive Center are also a part of this museum. The village grounds contain a windmill with a hand water pump, landscaped gardens, and a gazebo.

The Litschtalling Fall Festival held in September includes entertainment and ethnic foods.

129. WESTBROOK HERITAGE HOUSE MUSEUM 🅽🆁
First Street and Fourth, Westbrook, north of Highway 30.
507-274-6373

The Westbrook Heritage House Museum is located in a restored railroad depot. Originally the Chicago, St. Paul, Minneapolis, and Omaha depot, it was built in 1900 and used for passenger, livestock, and freight trains. The depot is a one-story wood-frame building with a hipped roof and large brackets under the eaves. The depot was added to the National Register of Historic Places in 1986. The railroad operated this depot until 1976, when the line running from Bingham Lake to Currie was closed.

The Depot Museum features train memorabilia, kitchen displays, children's items, and many other artifacts. An 1894 log cabin, originally located near Dutch Charley Creek, houses a museum of early pioneer life. The one-room cabin contains a sleeping loft and is constructed of wide, squared-off logs with tongue-and-groove corners.

The museum's special events include a pie social and a buffalo feed.

Westbrook Heritage House Museum log cabin, Westbrook

JACKSON COUNTY

130. FORT BELMONT

Hwy 71 South and County Road 34, Jackson.
Jackson Chamber of Commerce, 507-847-3867

Fort Belmont is a replica of a fort built to protect area settlers. Today it includes a replica stockade, mill, the 1902 Delafield Lutheran Church, an 1873 farmhouse, a recreated sod house, log cabin, blacksmith shop, and moonshine still.

Fort Belmont, three miles north of Jackson, was constructed and occupied by Norwegian settlers returning after the US-Dakota War of 1862. The hexagonal stockade originally surrounded a two-story log cabin. Classified as a civilian fort, eleven families occupied its stockade for nearly two years.

In 1958 the Watland family, descendants of fort inhabitants, created Fort Belmont Park with the construction of a stockade and a log cabin. The fort was opened to the public as a tourist attraction. When Interstate 90 opened in 1973, a group of citizens bought land near the interstate for a new site. In 1990 the fort was relocated and renovated.

The Lysgard Home and Summer Kitchen were moved to Fort Belmont Park in 2000 from the Wilder area. In 1873, after Norwegian immigrants Andrew and Mary Lysgard had lived in a dugout-sod home, they built the center section of a new wood-frame house, and several additions followed. Andrew and Mary raised three daughters in their home, and Lysgard descendants lived in the home until 1958. A separate summer kitchen, built in 1900, was also moved to Fort Belmont.

The park hosts an annual Rendezvous in September, which features costumed interpreters, children's games, and rifle-shooting and axe-throwing competitions.

131. OLSON-STAABAKKEN CABIN

Jackson County Fairgrounds, Jackson, off County Road 51. 507-662-5505

The Jackson County Historical Society cares for several historic buildings, including a pioneer village located at the county fairgrounds. An early church, school, and other buildings are among the historic buildings preserved in this pioneer village.

The Olson-Staabakken log cabin was built before 1860 and now sits in Jackson's Ashley Park. The cabin was the former home of Norwegian settlers to Jackson County. The Jackson County Historical Society's main museum and library is located in Lakefield.

LAC QUI PARLE COUNTY

132. LAC QUI PARLE COUNTY
HISTORICAL SOCIETY MUSEUM

Lac Qui Parle County Fairgrounds, Madison, on Highway 75. 320-598-7678

The Lac Qui Parle County Historical Society Museum

consists of six buildings, including a museum, 1870s log cabin, 1887 schoolhouse, the Robert Bly Study, and a machinery exhibit building. The current museum was established in 1972 on the Lac Qui Parle County Fairgrounds on the edge of Madison.

The cabin is built out of large elm and cottonwood logs fitted together with tongue-and-groove corner-construction methods. Nels Hantho built the cabin in 1870 with assistance from the owner, Harvor Flaa. One of the first buildings in the county, this building was used as Hantho Township's first schoolhouse in 1880–82.

The blue cottage, called the Robert Bly Study, is where Bly, a Madison native widely recognized for writing and translating poems and books, worked from the late 1950s through the 1970s. The cottage contains personal artifacts and a display of Bly's books.

Special events at the history center include a spring open house, summer Heritage Days, the annual meeting in the fall, and a Christmas program.

LINCOLN COUNTY

133. LINCOLN COUNTY PIONEER MUSEUM
610 Elm West, Hendricks, off County Road 17.
507-275-3537

The Lincoln County Pioneer Museum was established in 1969 when the Chicago and Northwestern Railroad discontinued railroad service to Hendricks and offered the early-twentieth-century depot for sale at auction. The Creative Coterie Federated Club and the Lincoln County Historical Society purchased the depot for $306 and paid $1,500 to move it to its present location.

Other buildings on the museum grounds include an 1879 country school, two modern museum buildings, and the 1925 Icelandic Church, which retains its original pews and altar fonts. In 1879 the first Icelandic immigrants to the county established a congregation with thirty-two charter members. Their first church was built in 1889 but destroyed by fire. This second church was built in 1925 and used until 1966, when the congregation disbanded.

Reverend J. J. Eske's Sears & Roebuck kit house was built in 1918 by Henry Lokken. Lokken's labor cost $1,500 and the materials $2,500. The house was originally located five miles west of Hendricks.

The two-and-one-half-story house is an American foursquare with nine rooms, a walk-up attic, screened-in front porch, and second-story rear sleeping porch. The wood-sided home features an open wooden staircase and all the original interior woodwork. The living room has the electric organ from Wilno Catholic Church; the dining room table is fully set with linens and china; and the kitchen contains a Sanico-brand range from the early-twentieth century. One room in the home is used to display quilts and another is the children's room featuring early toys and clothing. Two of the bedrooms are fully furnished, and another room is displayed as the reverend's study.

134. SNYDER LOG CABIN
Hole-in-the-Mountain Park, Lake Benton.
507-368-4480 or 507-368-9577

The 1862 log cabin located in Hole-in-the-Mountain Park was built by John Snyder, the first settler to purchase land in the area. The cabin is the only structure remaining from the first pioneer settlement in Lake Benton's Snyder's Flats area.

This prairie valley is located at the headwaters of Flandreau Creek, which runs toward the Big Sioux River. Native Americans called this half-mile-wide valley "Mountain Pass" or "Hole-in-the-Mountain." Today Hole-in-the-Mountain Preserve is a large remnant of the prairie owned and managed by The Nature Conservancy.

In 1888 this area was the site of the Grand Army of the Republic (GAR) Civil War Encampment, at which time over 5,000 visitors came to Lake Benton by train from across the Midwest for a reunion of Civil War soldiers.

In August the park hosts the "Benton Fremont Days" celebration, which features muzzle-loading shoots, historic games, and food.

LYON COUNTY

135. LYON COUNTY HISTORICAL SOCIETY MUSEUM
114 Third Street North, Marshall. 507-537-6580

The modern Lyon County Historical Museum's displays include an authentic 1950s Schwan's Dairy ice cream counter and soda fountain, a prairie schooner, Native American artifacts, and a complete 1872 log cabin.

Peter Flume built this cabin in 1872 in Lyon County's Northland Township, living in a dugout shelter until the cabin's completion. In 1873 the first election in Northland Township was held in this cabin. The Marshall Boy Scouts Troop dismantled the cabin and moved it to the museum from the county fairgrounds in 1994. A canvas roof was used in the reconstruction of the cabin, instead of a wooden roof, to display an authentic, albeit temporary, roofing material used by early settlers.

136. WHEELS ACROSS THE PRAIRIE MUSEUM
Highway 14, west of Tracy. 507-629-3661

Wheels Across the Prairie Museum portrays the history of the American railroad and the settling of the Minnesota prairies. An original Chicago Northwestern train depot from Volga, South Dakota, became the centerpiece of the museum. Authentic buildings moved to the site include an early post office, barbershop, and a blacksmith shop.

A fully outfitted original summer kitchen displays an early stove, utensils, and laundry equipment. The 1890 Monroe Township town hall was used as a school-

Wheels Across the Prairie Museum, Tracy

house until 1954, and is fully furnished with early school artifacts. A 1930s railroad serviceman's cottage displays donations of household artifacts, including an early stove, Hoosier cabinet, kitchen utensils, dining room table, buffet, and secretary. The living room contains a fainting couch and a Victrola. The bedroom has a Jenny Lind bed set and early quilts.

A one-and-one-half-story log cabin was moved to this location in 2001. Restoration added new glass windows and cedar shake shingles at the roof peaks. The Lowe family built the 1860s log cabin in the former Great Oasis Lake area in Murray County.

A 1915 American locomotive used in the yard of the St. Paul railroad system, a boxcar from the Chicago and Northwestern Railroad, and a caboose are located on the museum grounds. Other items of interest include early farm equipment, a 1906 auto bug, a 1928 oil pull-tractor, and a 1927 Studebacker.

MARTIN COUNTY

137. ORVILLE P. AND SARAH CHUBB HOUSE
209 Lake Avenue, Fairmont. 507-235-9777
or 1-800-657-3280

This house was built in 1867 for Orville P. Chubb, the first physician in Martin County, and his wife Sarah. In

1992 the Martin County Preservation Association purchased and restored the house, which is the oldest brick house still standing in Fairmont.

The bricks for the Greek Revival–style house were created out of clay from the banks of Buffalo Lake. The original front gable façade features a left-side doorway with a pedimented cornice. The centrally located window on the front façade of the house is topped by a second-story window, and both are accented with shutters. The wide band of trim at the gable end is painted white, as is the rest of the exterior wood trim. Originally consisting of three rooms, the house had one room added in 1930 and another section in 1935. Two bedrooms, one small child's room, and a bathroom are on the second floor.

The association hosts a fall stew dinner and a Christmas tea.

138. HERITAGE ACRES
827 Lake Avenue, Fairmont. 507-238-1563

Heritage Acres is also known as the South Central Minnesota Agricultural Interpretive Center. The land for the site is the former homestead of Reuben M. Ward, first settled in 1867 and given to the city by family members. In the early 1970s, the Heritage Acres organization formed to create a living-history farm museum. In 1981 the farmhouse, built in 1890, was donated by the Noble Nelson family and moved to this site.

The Nelson farmhouse is in the Upright-and-Wing style. Visitors enter through a side porch. The front façade of the house features a front gable on the second story with a bow window on the main floor. The entrance porch is located in the wing section of the house. The main floor includes the kitchen, dining room, and living room. The upstairs has three bedrooms, but no bathroom. The Nelson family used an outhouse until 1981.

A reconstructed red barn was built on the location of the original Ward family barn. The museum grounds also include a windmill, chicken coop, carriage shed, and wooden water tower. Other historical buildings moved to this site include an original blacksmith shop from south of Fairmont, the Welcome train depot, a school from near Trimont, and a church from the Welcome area.

Special events include a music festival in July, a threshing bee in August, and a harvest festival in October.

Heritage Acres, Fairmont

139. LIVINGSTON LOG CABIN

1300 North Avenue, Fairmont, in Lincoln Park.
507-238-9461

William Robert Livingston built this log cabin in 1865 in Silver Lake Township in Martin County. Called the Tall Oaks Farm, the original Livingston property still has many tall oaks along the lake's shoreline. In 1953, Alden and Helen Austin donated the cabin to the Martin County Historical Society, which arranged for the city of Fairmont to move the cabin to Lincoln Park.

The one-and-one-half-story cabin is in excellent condition for its age and features a central front door on the gable end of the cabin, a first-story window just left of the door, and a loft window centered above the door. The large, wide logs are squared and dovetailed at the corners. Inside, the cabin has one room and a loft. The furnishings include a cast-iron stove, a table and chairs, and an oil lamp.

MURRAY COUNTY

140. END-O-LINE PARK ℕℝ
440 Mill Street North (County Road 38), Currie.
507-763-3708

The End-O-Line Park began in 1972, when two leaders of Currie's 4-H Club decided to clean up the turntable in the railroad yard, purchased the abandoned Chicago and Northwestern depot for one dollar, and moved it across the highway. The turntable was added to the National Register of Historic Places in 1977. End-O-Line Park has also purchased and moved several authentic train-related structures to the park over the years. Authentic train cars include the Section Crew Cars, the 1923 Georgia Northern Steam Engine #102, the Brookville Diesel Switcher, and the 1942 Grand Trunk Western Caboose.

The park's historic buildings include the District 1 Schoolhouse, called the Sunrise School, and Currie's 1872 general store, which is stocked with vintage items from the original store. End-O-Line Park's section house was originally located in Comfrey. The Chicago and Northwestern Railway built the house in 1899 for a section foreman and his family. This restored New England saltbox-style structure features furnishings and artifacts from the early-twentieth century. The main floor contains a parlor, kitchen, bedroom, and a spare bedroom made into a dining room. The second story has two bedrooms for children, as well as an attic storage space.

Henry Hilfers built the Hilfers train yard here with a small depot, turntable, coal bunker, water tower, and engine with several cars. This miniature train yard is still in use for rides around the park. A scale model railroad, on display in the depot, reproduces the Currie railroad yards as they were in the early-twentieth century.

141. KOCH CABIN

163 State Park Road, Currie, off County Road 38.
507-763-3256

Andrew Koch built this log cabin in 1858. Originally located in the Shetek settlement four miles north of its current site in Lake Shetek State Park, the cabin is the oldest remaining building in Murray County.

The cabin has a violent history. The first documented murder in Murray County occurred here when Charley Waubau shot Bill Clark through the window. Koch was killed outside of his cabin on August 20, 1862, during the US-Dakota War. His wife was taken captive and later escaped. At the time of US-Dakota War, there were nine families' cabins in Shetek. Today, a marked trail traces the path of the fleeing settlers to a slough where more than a dozen settlers were killed during the 1862 attack.

The Koch cabin was used for a time as a vacation cottage at Tepeeota Resort. The Murray County Historical Society received the donated cabin in 1960 and moved it to this site in 1962. In 1998 care of the cabin was officially turned over to park staff.

142. WORNSON CABIN

2480 Twenty-Ninth Street, Murray County Fairgrounds,
Slayton. 507-836-6533

This log cabin on the grounds of the Murray County Historical Society Museum was built in 1872 by Ole and Martha Wornson. The couple and their children arrived in 1860 from Norway. They homesteaded a claim in Slayton Township, first living in a dugout. Family members used the cabin until 1951.

The historical society moved the cabin to the county fairgrounds in 1976. Constructed of squared oak logs with square nails, the one-and-one-half-story cabin has a sleeping loft and a lean-to addition. Today the cabin is furnished with an early table and chairs and a small cast-iron parlor stove.

The museum grounds also contain a Works Progress Administration–built round barn and the modern museum building that holds open houses in December and April and during the Murray County Fair in August.

NOBLES COUNTY

143. HISTORIC DAYTON HOUSE 🏠
1311 Fourth Avenue, Worthington. 507-727-1311

Designed by noted Sioux Falls architect Wallace Dow, the Dayton House was built for George Draper Dayton in 1890. It is a blend of Colonial and Georgian Revival styles, with Beaux Arts details and a widow's walk at the top of the house. The double front door is surrounded by leaded glass sidelights and topped by a leaded glass transom window. The front porch's Ionic columns are original. Restoration of the home was funded by the Dayton family, the Target Corporation, and other private citizens. The house was added to the National Register of Historic Places in 2004.

A New York native, the hard-working Dayton was given a tip to purchase farmland in Worthington. When Dayton journeyed to Worthington to survey his investments, he asked friends and families to invest in more property with him, and his investments eventually allowed him to take over the Bank of Worthington. In Worthington he ran six businesses including a flourmill and railroad, and he served on the school board. The Daytons raised four children, David Draper, Caroline, George Nelson, and Josephine.

Although he pursued investments in Minneapolis, Dayton supervised them from Worthington. In 1902 he loaned money to two men for the Goodfellow Daylight Store. When he bought them out, the business became Dayton's Drygood Company. Dayton eventually moved to Minneapolis, building a home similar to this one on Blaisdell Avenue.

Historic Dayton House, Worthington
(Historic Dayton House, Inc.)

The Worthington home's second owner was Florence Moulton Smallwood, whose son-in-law Jack Cashel became a judge and state senator. In the 1930s the Cashels bought the Dayton house from the Smallwoods. Cashel's second wife, Ruth, later took in boarders and eventually turned the home into the Cashel Nursing Home, which operated from the mid-1940s until 1983.

The house's front entrance hall features encaustic tiles and wood floors with inlaid details, which continue throughout the house. On the main floor, double pocket doors separate the public rooms, and all of the leaded glass windows and fireplace mantels are original to the home. The home was custom-built to suit Dayton's small stature, and the height of windows, stair railings, and doorknobs were adjusted accordingly. The parlor, library, and dining room serve as a showcase for the museum's collections of items from the Dayton, Smallwood, and Cashel families.

The multiuse Dayton House hosts private functions, and second floor suites lodge bed-and-breakfast guests.

144. NOBLES COUNTY PIONEER VILLAGE

1600 Stower Drive, Worthington, at Nobles County Fairgrounds. 507-376-3125 or 507-376-4431

Nobles County Pioneer Village is adjacent to the Nobles County Fairgrounds. The village contains more than forty historic buildings moved to the museum from across the county. Historic houses include a small parsonage, two wood-frame farmhouses, a replica sod house, a train depot, gas station, hospital, blacksmith shop, fire station, and school. A modern museum contains exhibits of early farm machinery and other artifacts.

This village comes to life each year during the Nobles County Fair with costumed volunteers. The museum also hosts the Prairie Power Reapers Reunion in mid-August and Christmas events.

PIPESTONE COUNTY

145. C. O. CHRISTIANSON HOUSE

208 Second Street East, Jasper. 507-348-8946 or 507-348-3963

This structure was built in 1888 to serve as a home and store for C. O. Christianson. The front of the building is the store, with the original counter and shelves. The back room has a table, stove, side door, butter churn and crock, and narrow stairs leading to Christianson's sleeping loft. The building was moved from its original location in 1981, causing it to lose its place on the National Register of Historic Places. The house is operated by the Jasper Historical Society.

The Jasper Historical Society museum is located downtown on Wall Street and features historical artifacts from the Jasper area.

The Jasper Historical Society holds a supper benefit during the yearly Jasper celebration and occasionally offers Christmas tours.

C. O. Christianson House, Jasper

REDWOOD COUNTY

146. GILFILLAN ESTATE

Highway 67, between Redwood Falls and Morgan.
507-249-3451 or 507-249-2210

Charles Duncan Gilfillan established this large farmstead
in the 1880s. The house and farm were added to the
National Register of Historic Places in 1980.

Gilfillan, born in New York in 1831, studied law
and moved to Minnesota, where he became a partner in
the St. Paul Water Company, which was then a private
enterprise. He sold the company to the city of St. Paul
in 1882, then sold his Ramsey County property and purchased 13,000 acres of land in Redwood County. Here
he built this large home and office, a grain elevator,
stockyard, and tenant homes. His son, Charles Oswin
Gilfillan, born in 1872, succeeded his father as owner of
the estate. C.O. died in 1962, and farm acreage was sold
off. After the death of his wife, Anna, descendants gave
the property to the Redwood County Historical Society.

Visitors to the home enter through the modernized kitchen in the far rear corner of the house, which is adjacent to the dining room. The dining room features a fireplace, Tiffany chandelier, and French doors leading to the rest of the house. The family's mix of antique and modern furniture and updates to the living areas create the house's eclectic feel.

On the second story, the large master bedroom displays son Charles's tuxedo and his wife's 1920s wedding "going away" outfit. Two smaller bedrooms, a bath, and two small maid's quarters are also on this floor.

Original farm buildings house a collection of antique farm equipment. A pergola connects the rear kitchen entrance to Charles's office, which features family portraits, his desk, and a fireplace. The icehouse and water tower are original to the 1880s farmstead.

147. LOWER SIOUX AGENCY 🏛 Ⓝ
County Highway 2, nine miles east of Redwood Falls.
507-697-6321

In the 1850s the Lower Sioux Agency was the yearly distribution center for money and goods owed to the Mdewakanton and Wahpekute bands of the Dakota as part of their treaties with the US government. The complex was home not only to the tribe, but also to agency employees, traders, teachers, and missionaries.

By 1860 the government village probably housed more than one hundred employees in fifteen to twenty buildings. Buildings at the site included stables and storehouses, a blacksmith shop, cookhouse, school, and living quarters. Nearby there were more than one hundred brick, wood-frame, and log homes built for the Dakota residents living and farming on the site. Their villages were located along the bluff overlooking the Minnesota River. At the western edge of the agency were four trading posts.

In the summer of 1862, the agency was destroyed during the US-Dakota War. A crop failure and late annuity payments contributed to the crisis, as well as tension between the Dakota, government workers, and the traders because of the government's failure to fulfill the provisions of the treaties. The Lower Sioux Agency was the site of the first organized Indian attack in the 1862 US-Dakota War.

Today, a stone warehouse built in 1861 is all that remains of the original agency buildings. By 1866 the US government began selling the agency site's land to individual settlers. August Knueppel settled the land containing the warehouse remains in 1881 and remodeled the building to become his family's home.

Lower Sioux Agency, Redwood Falls

The cobblestone warehouse exhibits a construction method rarely seen in Minnesota. Presumably John Nairn, the carpenter working at the agency, planned and supervised construction of the building. Large stone quoins form the corners of this simple Greek Revival building. A stone plaque over a second-story window has inscribed the year "1861" and the initials "T. J. G." for agent Thomas J. Galbraith.

In 1967 the Minnesota Historical Society purchased the warehouse and agency site, later restoring the warehouse to its original appearance. An interpretive center was built in 1970, the year the Lower Sioux Agency site was added to the National Register of Historic Places. In 1971 the Minnesota state legislature established the Lower Sioux Agency Historic District.

A trail circles around the area where the traders set up their posts and homes, and the grounds feature period gardens with heirloom plants. A cemetery contains the grave of Andrew Robertson, an agency worker who died in 1859, along with the graves of some members of the Knueppel family.

Many special events are held at the site through cooperation between the Lower Sioux Community and the Minnesota Historical Society.

148. LAURA INGALLS WILDER MUSEUM
330 Eighth Street, Walnut Grove, near Highway 14.
1-800-528-7280

The Laura Ingalls Wilder Museum, established in 1974, honors the popular "Little House" books author. Tourists travel from around the world to see the sites mentioned in her books.

The Ingalls family lived in this area on a farmstead near Walnut Grove from 1874 until 1876. Laura based her book *On the Banks of Plum Creek* on this time in her life. The Ingalls family first lived in a dugout house built along the banks of Plum Creek, now a marked site where tall grass prairie grows. Later, from 1877 until 1879, the Ingalls family lived in a house in the town of Walnut Grove. Today visitors can visit the sites in town associated with the family.

Laura Ingalls Wilder Museum, Walnut Grove

The Laura Ingalls Wilder museum has several historic buildings on its grounds, including an 1898 railroad depot, an 1880s school, and a recreated chapel. The depot houses an exhibit titled "Laura's Room," which showcases personal memorabilia. Also on display are items from the actors and actresses of the "Little House on the Prairie" TV series. Another room details the founding and establishment of the village of Walnut Grove.

The museum grounds also contain an 1890s house originally built by August and Clara Hult. This small Victorian house features an onion-shaped dome turret reminiscent of the domes on Russian orthodox churches. The house's kitchen, parlor, and bedroom contain items from the 1890s through 1920s. This home, referred to as "Grandma's House," displays the more than 250 dolls collected by Beulah Kelton from the 1870s through the 1900s. Another house on the museum grounds, the Nelson House, is also open to the public. The Heritage Lane building features a covered wagon, early tools and farm machinery, and equipment from the original Walnut Grove Tribune newspaper office.

In July the city of Walnut Grove becomes the site of the Wilder Pageant, and an outdoor play based on Laura's life as detailed in her books is presented. The festival also includes performances of country, bluegrass, and folk music at the outdoor amphitheater.

RENVILLE COUNTY

149. FORT RIDGELY HISTORY CENTER 🏛
72404 County Road 30, Fairfax, in Fort Ridgely State Park.
507-426-7888

Fort Ridgely was built between 1853 and 1855 as a government outpost for keeping the peace as new settlers arrived to stake their claims in lands that had belonged to the Dakota before the 1851 Treaties of Traverse Des Sioux

Fort Ridgely History Center, Fairfax *(Joe Michel/MHS)*

and Mendota had forced the Dakota to sell their land and move to a government-created reservation. This fort was named "Ridgely" in honor of three men of the same name who had died during the Mexican War. The fort also became a training base for Civil War volunteers.

During the summer of 1862 a long-simmering conflict between the Dakota, the US government, and the new settlers erupted. Dakota warriors attacked Fort Ridgely twice during the US-Dakota War. Nearly 300 soldiers and civilians defended the fort until Army reinforcements ended the siege.

The fort closed in 1872, and local farmers used the buildings for storing crops. The land was purchased in 1896 to create a war memorial to those who fought in the US-Dakota War. In 1911 more land was purchased and the site was designated a state park.

Today visitors can tour the Fort Ridgely Historic Site, owned by the Minnesota Historical Society and operated by the Nicollet County Historical Society. The restored stone commissary serves as a visitor center, which has exhibits that portray the history of the fort history and the war. The original log powder house has also been restored. Foundation remnants of other original buildings are marked. Visitors may also tour the fort's cemetery.

Special events are held on summer weekends.

150. LERUD CABIN

441 North Park Drive, Morton, near Highway 19.
507-697-6147

The Renville County Historical Society Museum complex has seven buildings, including two 1885 country schools, an exhibit building, a blacksmith shop, a machine and tool display building, an 1869 Scandinavian immigrant log cabin, and an 1891 church.

The Lerud family log cabin, built in 1869, is furnished with period artifacts. Embret and Mary Lerud built this cabin in Sacred Heart Township. The cabin was moved to the museum site in 1953 and restored. The construction methods are typical of those used by early Scandinavian pioneers.

ROCK COUNTY

151. HINKLY HOUSE MUSEUM Ⓝ

217 Freeman Avenue North, Luverne, near Highway 75.
507-449-2115

The 1892 Ray Benjamin (R. B.) Hinkly house was built of red Sioux quartzite from Hinkly's own quarry, which is now part of Blue Mounds State Park. The stone wall on the east side of the house and the stone lions gracing the front steps were created by Knute Steine, a Norwegian immigrant and master stonecutter.

R. B. Hinkly, born in Clermont, Iowa, in 1860, arrived in Luverne in 1882 to organize the Rock County Bank, of which he later became president. He married Mary Harrington, and they had four children. Hinkly owned a quarry, an advertising company, an insurance firm, and farm and ranch land in Minnesota and Texas, and he was involved in banking in Luverne and elsewhere. He also pioneered irrigation systems and established the citrus industry on his truck farms in the Rio Grande Valley near San Benito, Texas. Additionally,

Hinkly House Museum, Luverne

he served as mayor of Luverne for several terms and was involved in county organizations.

Hinkly's second wife lived in the home until 1955. Descendants gave the house to the city to be used by the Rock County Historical Society. The museum was established in 1959, and the house was added to the National Register of Historic Places in 1975.

The architectural style of the house is a blend of Queen Anne and Richardsonian Romanesque. The exterior features double-front gables, side gables on the third story, and a fourth-story gable with narrow "eyebrow" windows. The gable details contain fish-scale and cross-paned paneled trim, and the porch gable has a carved frieze. Jasper quartzite was used as a header stone above the windows.

The twelve-room house had all the advanced plumbing and electrical systems available in the 1890s, being wired for electricity and having indoor plumbing even before it was available in town. Throughout the main floor rooms, windows contain leaded and stained glass imported from England.

Hinkly personally assisted in the building of the house. He designed and helped to lay the parquet flooring in the foyer. All the woodwork, including the wainscoting, pocket doors, and paneled staircase, was created for the house in Hinkly's basement workshop.

The library and six upstairs rooms were redecorated in 2002. During the redecorating process an original stencil was uncovered in one of the bedrooms when the wallpaper was removed, and this stenciling has been re-created on the walls in the room.

Christmas tours and teas are among the special events held at the house, and an "Angel Tea" benefits a local hospice.

152. FREDERICK MANFRED HOUSE
US Highway 75, north of Luverne. 507-283-1307

For many years Blue Mounds State Park's Interpretive Center was located in the former home of popular regional novelist Frederick Feikema Manfred. Manfred's stories were often set in the Great Plains. His "Siouxland" stories brought this area of the world to life. Manfred, born in Iowa, lived in Minnesota and taught in South Dakota. He is the author of many books in the Western genre, including *Morning Red, Conquering Horse*, and *Wanderlust*.

Manfred's modern home is built out of Sioux quartzite with glass windows as walls. The house has a second-story lookout peak and a glassed-in porch with an exposed rock wall and fireplace inside. A wrought-iron railing separates the interior rock wall and fireplace from the sunken area in the glassed-in porch. Custom wrought-iron detailing includes a peace pipe crossing an arrow. One wing has the kitchen, bath, and dining room with fireplace, and the other wing housed the bedrooms. The house's interior is currently closed to the public because of state budget cuts. Information about Manfred can be found on plaques located outside the house.

Frederick Manfred House, Luverne

Other historic structures in the park, which features 100-foot sandstone cliffs and roaming buffalo, include two dams and a sanitation building built by the Works Progress Administration in the 1930s. The park's unique mystery is a 1,250-foot man-made ridge of rocks that runs in an east-west direction and lines up with the sunrise and sunset on the first day of spring and autumn. The origin of this stone feature is unknown.

WANTONWAN COUNTY

153. ASHIPPUN POST OFFICE CABIN
423 Dill Avenue SW, Madelia. 507-642-3247 or 507-642-8183

Halvor Knudson Barland and his family immigrated to Wisconsin from Kragero, Norway, in 1853. The family moved by an ox-drawn covered wagon to Rosendale Township and built this cabin in 1857. The building has been rebuilt inside the modern Wantonwan County Historical Society Museum.

The cabin was used not only as a family home, but also as a church, meeting house, and the Ashippun post office. The family survived two raids by Dakota tribe members.

The cabin, which was given to the local Daughters of the American Revolution chapter in 1925, was moved to Flanders Park in Madelia and again in 1974 to its current home. The rebuilt cabin has been completely restored and furnished with period artifacts.

154. VOSS PARK
*Butterfield, north of Highway 60. 507-956-2040
or 507-359-2846*

The Butterfield Threshing Association created the collection of historical buildings at Voss Park, where the association holds its annual Butterfield Threshing Bee. A. R. Voss donated the land to create a city park.

Authentic buildings moved to the site include a late-nineteenth-century schoolhouse from near Odin, an early-twentieth-century Presbyterian Church, the Granada depot, and a farmhouse with a detached summer kitchen built by Russian Mennonites who held their first church services in the house. The white one-and-one-half-story house has gingerbread trim on the porch and exterior stairs to the half-story.

A recreated town includes a barbershop, shoe repair shop, harness shop, general store, and drug store, all of which house original furnishings and fixtures from Butterfield shops. The Threshing Association has constructed a reproduction of Tuberg's Gristmill, the first mill in the area. The flour bin is a recreated building, and the barn, granary, and outhouse are original buildings moved to this site from Tuberg's mill, which operated between 1877 and 1905. The restored 1875 Larson log cabin was found south of Butterfield during a farmhouse remodeling and moved to this site.

YELLOW MEDICINE COUNTY

155. LUND-HOEL HOUSE ⓝⓡ
101 Fourth Street, Canby, at Highway 75 (St. Olaf Avenue).
507-223-7371 or 507-223-5613

This 1891 landmark house was originally a modest Victorian wood-frame house built for John Grant and Flora Miller Lund. With his growing wealth, Lund remodeled the house in 1900 into a larger Queen Anne–style home, adding a front porch with stone balustrades and an onion-dome tower, as well as a large addition on the rear of the home.

John G. Lund, who started the Lund Land Agency in 1888 at age twenty, quickly became a millionaire as he bought and sold large tracts of land in this booming prairie town. He was elected mayor of Canby in 1889. In 1902 Lund started the First National Bank of Canby with his brothers and other investors, and one year later he moved with his wife to Minneapolis to operate his land business's main office. In 1905 he was elected to the Minnesota legislature.

Lund sold his Canby house to Rev. Olaf and Mary Lund Hoel, his brother-in-law and sister, in 1903. One of their children, Nella Hoel Berg, owned the house from 1928 until 1958. Bill and Minnie Richter bought the house in 1958 and operated a board-and-care center there until 1975, when MECCA (Museum Encompassing the Canby Community Area) bought the house for $18,000. The John G. Lund House was added to the National Register of Historic Places in 1978.

During restoration some of the original gingerbread trim, gas lighting fixtures, and the bathtub were found and restored. The house was repainted to match the colors used when the Lunds first remodeled the house.

The front door has its original stained glass. A music room, parlor, and dining room as well as an original bathroom are on the main floor. One upstairs bedroom is open to the nursery, which features antique children's items. Other rooms include a study and several bed-rooms. The MECCA Interpretive Center is located in a recreated carriage house on the property. The structure has the cupola salvaged from the original building.

156. UPPER SIOUX AGENCY 🏠
5908 Highway 67, Granite Falls. 320-564-4777

The Upper Sioux Agency Historic Site was originally part of the Upper Sioux (Yellow Medicine) Indian Agency. The Minnesota Historical Society maintains the historic site in conjunction with the Department of Natural Resources. The historic site, listed on the National Register of Historic Places in 1970, is located within Upper Sioux Agency State Park, which was established in 1963 to preserve and interpret the former Agency site and the Upper Sioux Agency Historic Site.

After the Treaties of Mendota and Traverse Des Sioux in 1851, Dakota tribe members from Iowa and Minnesota were moved to a reservation in this area along the Minnesota River Valley. The Yellow Medicine Agency, now referred to as the Upper Sioux Agency, was created in 1854 to oversee the terms of the treaty.

By 1862 the Upper Sioux Agency consisted of a two-story warehouse with offices for the agent and a doctor, a jail, two employee duplexes, a manual labor school, a bake house and oven, and at least one barn. Beyond this cluster of brick buildings were more wood-frame homes for agency employees, a brick kiln, and a sawmill and gristmills, as well as four trading posts. About one hundred Dakota families lived at this site. They constructed their brick homes with assistance from the agency farmer. In 1862 the Upper Sioux Agency was destroyed during the US-Dakota War.

At the site today is a reconstructed employee duplex from the 1854 Agency, which is currently not open to the public. The original duplex house, built in 1859–60, was burned but not wholly destroyed in 1862. After the war, the land was reclaimed by the US government and sold to individual settlers. The George Olds family settled a portion of this land and made the duplex their home. Olds reconstructed the remains of the duplex in the late 1860s into a one-and-one-half-story building with dormers. He also rebuilt the remains of the original barn. In the 1970s the Minnesota Historical Society reconstructed the collapsing duplex. Ruins in the park include the cellar depressions of the sawmill and marked foundations of the wood houses built before the agency's kiln was operating. The buildings' sites have historical markers, and visitors can take a self-guided walking tour of the site.

157. ANDREW J. VOLSTEAD HOUSE [NR]
163 Ninth Avenue, Granite Falls, near Highway 23/212.
320-564-3011 or 320-564-2255

This house was the residence of Andrew J. Volstead from 1894 until 1930. Volstead served as a US congressman for ten terms beginning in 1902. He co-authored the Capper-Volstead Act of 1922, which legalized collective farm-produce marketing. Volstead also wrote the "National Prohibition Enforcement Act" of 1919, popularly known as the "Volstead Act," which led to the implementation of prohibition.

Volstead attended St. Olaf College in Northfield and Decorah Institute in Decorah, Iowa. He studied and practiced law there and then settled in Granite Falls in 1886, where he served as mayor and county district attorney. Volstead also helped establish the Granite Falls hydroelectric power cooperative. After leaving public office, he worked for a time in St. Paul as a legal advisor for a prohibition enforcement agency, but returned to Granite Falls, where he lived until his death in 1947.

Volstead's 1878 Italianate house features a squared tower with a pyramid-shaped roof. The tower, located where the house's two wings join, was an addition to

the house while Volstead and his family lived here.
The main floor of the house includes the formal parlor,
family parlor, dining room, and a back room that was
a kitchen. Volstead most likely used the front parlor as
his office. Family artifacts in the house include a rocking
chair, secretary's desk, and some traveling trunks. There
is original oak woodwork on the main floor, with an al-
ternating light and dark stained pattern in the flooring.
A leaded glass window graces the east side of the tower
along the staircase to the second floor.

The house continued to be a private residence after
Volstead died in 1947. It was purchased by the Minne-
sota Association of Cooperatives and given to the city of
Granite Falls in 1979 to create a museum in Volstead's
honor. The house was added to the National Register of
Historic Places in 1974, and it was deemed a National
Historic Landmark in 1976. Today the house is used for
multiple purposes, and plaques offer information on
Volstead's career.

Andrew J. Volstead House, Granite Falls

158. YELLOW MEDICINE COUNTY HISTORICAL MUSEUM
Highway 23 and Highway 67, Granite Falls. 320-564-4479

The modern Yellow Medicine County Historical Museum houses exhibits focusing on local history. On the museum's grounds are two historic log cabins, which are not open to the public for touring.

The museum was closed for a time following a devastating flood in 1997 and reopened in 2000. The future is uncertain for this site because Granite Falls is redeveloping its riverfront properties due to repeated flooding.

Historic Bunnell House, Homer

SOUTHEAST REGION

SOUTHEAST

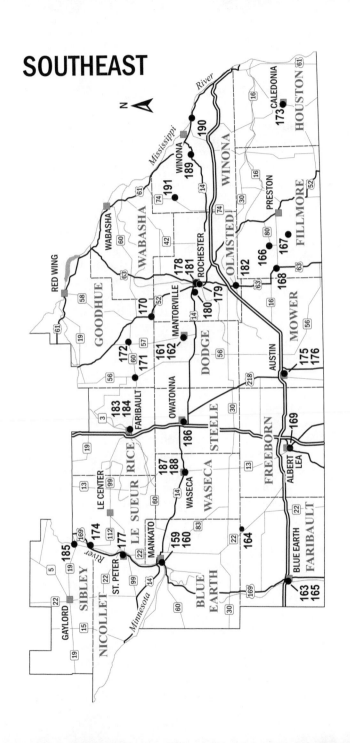

BLUE EARTH COUNTY

159. HUBBARD HOUSE Ⓝ

606 Broad Street South, Mankato. 507-345-5566

This elegant house was built in 1871 for Rensselaer D. Hubbard, founder of the Hubbard Milling Company in Mankato. In 1938, the Blue Earth County Historical Society purchased the R. D. Hubbard House and then deeded it to the city of Mankato to create a museum. The house first opened for tours in 1938. It was added to the National Register of Historic Places in 1976.

The Blue Earth County Historical Society used the house for its exhibit galleries, artifact storage, offices, and research center for more than forty years. When the new Heritage Center opened in 1990, the society began restoring the house to interpret the life of the Hubbard family in the home in the year 1905.

The French Second Empire house features a mansard roof, a front porch with Ionic columns, and a telescoped rear addition in the Italianate style. It is mainly crafted of brick, with Mankato stone trim details. The Hubbards first remodeled the house in the 1880s and later again in 1905. The carriage house was built in 1891 in the Queen Anne style, and today it displays a 1916 fire engine.

The front foyer leads to an open hallway with a dramatic staircase in the center. On the right is the formal parlor with recreated ceiling frescoes that match the designs in the original wool carpet, a Bacon Raven rosewood piano, and Quezal light fixtures. Across the hall is the library, where brown damask fabric on the walls gives the room a masculine feel. The brown-patterned carpet is original, and the painted ceilings have been restored. The library connects to the dining room. This room features a round cherry table beneath a dramatic Tiffany chandelier. The dining room connects to the kitchen, separated by a butler's pantry. The back of the central hall leads to the kitchen as well as Hubbard's rear office. This room has a separate outside door that allowed business associates to enter directly into the office. The reconstructed 1873 Holberg Cabin is located in the Hubbard house basement.

Saturday afternoons at the Hubbard House in the summer feature garden tours, teas, fashion shows, and themed Victorian events. The house is decorated for the holidays in December.

The Blue Earth County Historical Society Heritage Center is just up the hill from the museum on Cherry Street. The Heritage Center is home to displays of local historical artifacts and interactive exhibits. The historical society's archives and research rooms are also located in this center. Many special events are held at the Heritage Center for the general public, and for families with children.

160. MAUD HART LOVELACE CHILDHOOD HOME AND TACY'S HOUSE

332 and 333 Center Street, Mankato. 507-345-8103

The Betsy-Tacy Society preserves the real geographical places fictionalized in the popular "Betsy-Tacy" series of children's books written by Maud Hart Lovelace about her childhood in Mankato, the fictionalized "Deep Valley." Ten Betsy-Tacy books were published between 1940 and 1955, followed by three more "Deep Valley" books.

The society owns Tacy's house at 332 Center Street, the childhood home of Frances "Bick" Kenney Kirch, fictionalized as Betsy's best friend Tacy Kelly. Currently

Maud Hart Lovelace's "Tacy's House," Mankato (*Betsy-Tacy Society*)

Tacy's house serves as headquarters for society activities.

Lovelace gave the character she based on herself the name "Betsy." Betsy's house is across the street at 333 Center Street. This was the house where Maud Hart Lovelace grew up. The society purchased this house in 2001.

Both houses had fallen victim to "remuddling" since the Hart and Kenney families lived in the homes. The exterior of Tacy's house had aluminum siding, shutters, and an added enclosed front porch. Exterior renovations have brought back the white wood siding and opened up both porches of this Upright-and-Wing house. The house features a front gable with two single windows on the main floor level and a joined pair of windows on the second story. An Italianate-style bowed window has been restored, as has a rear kitchen porch. Betsy's house still retains the original wood siding, which has been recently repainted. The house is in the same Upright-and-Wing style as Tacy's. Fundraising to restore both homes continues.

The Betsy-Tacy Society holds a Halloween party, a book festival in November, and an annual Christmas event.

DODGE COUNTY

161. DODGE COUNTY HISTORICAL SOCIETY
615 Main Street North, Mantorville. 507-635-5508

The Dodge County Historical Society is housed in the 1869 St. John's Episcopal Church. The building, constructed of locally quarried limestone, was designed using architectural sketches drawn by Sir Christopher Wren, who was knighted for his design of St. Paul's Church in London, England. Sara A. Ruth, the wife of the church's first pastor Peter Ruth, left provisions in her will to build the church. She died in 1866, and the church was built over her grave.

Today the church displays the Dodge County Historical Society's collections. On the museum grounds are two other historic structures that were moved to this site. The "Little Red House on the Hill," a red wood-frame house built in 1856, features a front porch and window trim painted white. George and Thrine Bourdon restored the small house. The grounds also hold an 1883 rural school.

The museum is part of the Marigold Days festival in September and other special events.

162. MANTORVILLE RESTORATION HOUSE
Main Street North (Highway 57), Mantorville.
507-269-8704 or 507-635-5464

This 1856 house served as the first Dodge County courthouse and jail from 1858 until 1965. The Mantorville Restoration Association acquired the two-story folk Victorian house that features an open front porch with a turned spindle balustrade and a decorated gable. The front of the house displays a gabled façade with two windows.

The front porch entrance to the house leads to the parlor. An alcove displays a pump organ donated by the Hubbell House. The dining room has a pulley-operated light fixture over the center table and chairs, a china hutch, a wicker buggy, and a bentwood cradle. The kitchen includes the original Home Jewel–brand cast-iron stove that was shipped here from Detroit, and a pie-safe with punched tin details on its doors. The main floor also includes a bathroom added in the late-nineteenth century, a side foyer, and a small exterior porch. A drop-leaf desk and chairs used by jurors when the house was a courthouse are displayed in the foyer.

On the second story, visitors view the former bedrooms, which display quilts, antique clothing, children's toys, World War I objects, and early cameras. From the outside of the house an exterior door leads to the basement, where the old jail cell still exists.

Also on the property is an 1850s log cabin, once home to the brewmaster of the Ginsburg Brewery. The association purchased this cabin in 1985 and spent several years restoring it. The association also gives tours of a restored 1860s Carriage House in Mantorville and recently received ownership of the town's 1918 opera house, where restoration is currently in progress.

FARIBAULT COUNTY

163. HISTORY LANE
*Faribault County Fairgrounds, Blue Earth, near Interstate 90.
507-526-5421*

The restored buildings on History Lane, maintained by the Faribault County Historical Society, include the Woodland schoolhouse, the Guckeen post office, the West Delavan Lutheran Church, the Krosch Log House, a windmill, and a blacksmith shop. The antique machinery shed houses a collection of farming implements and a gas station.

The two-story Krosch Log Cabin built in 1862 by Casper Lampman was originally located in Elmore. German immigrants Augustus and Emma Krosch were the home's next owners. They raised eleven children in the cabin and lived in it for thirty-four years. The cabin remained in the family until 1910. The building was then used for storage until Jay and Frances Hickle donated it to the Faribault County Historical Society, and it was moved to the fairgrounds in 1985.

The first floor living area contains a cook stove, washing machine, log chair, cupboard, butter churn, and early kitchen utensils. There is a white iron bed, a Singer treadle sewing machine, and a floor loom here as well. The second story has two bedrooms separated by a narrow hall.

The site hoses an antique tractor pull and bluegrass concert during the fair, and the society sponsors an ice cream social during Green Giant Days in June.

164. KREMER HOUSE
317 Main Street, Minnesota Lake. 507-462-3420

This large brick Queen Anne house was built for Peter Kremer and his wife Millie in 1902. Peter's brothers, Nicholas J., John, and John P., were among the earliest settlers of Minnesota Lake. Peter Kremer moved to Minnesota Lake in 1874, where he played an active part in business and public affairs. He was a mayor, owned a mill, and worked as a banker and civic developer.

After the Kremers' deaths, the house was divided, rented out, and left vacant for several years. It was scheduled for demolition, but a group of citizens began work to save it. In 1980 the house was added to National Register of Historic Places. After restoration was completed in 1986, the house was

Kremer House, Minnesota Lake

opened to the public as a joint space for the library and the historical society.

Pairs of columns and turned spindles form the home's front porch. The front façade of the second floor has a set of three windows with limestone sills. The gabled third story of the home features a decorative cornice over a set of squared windows along with decorative wooden panels. A three-story turret characteristic of the Queen Anne style is located on the dining room side of the house. The turret features curved-glass windows and is topped with a conical roof and a finial.

Today, bookcases line the walls of rooms formerly used as the dining room, study, and formal parlor. Items of local historical interest are displayed throughout the house. An oak Empire Revival–style fireplace in the front parlor features a surround with decorative Ionic columns and a beveled mirror above the hearth. Upstairs are a quilt exhibit and a veteran's room. On display is a set of dishes from the Kremer family, as well as a washbasin, bowl, and chamber set decorated with a rose pattern and gold trim.

Special events include book talks and teas.

165. JAMES B. WAKEFIELD HOUSE [NR]

405 Sixth Street East, Blue Earth, at Ramsey Street South.
507-526-5421

James B. Wakefield, one of Blue Earth's founders, built this Italianate house in 1868. Wakefield was an attorney and a principal organizer of Faribault County. He later served two terms as lieutenant governor of Minnesota and two terms in the US House of Representatives. This house, the oldest remaining residential structure in Blue Earth, is operated by the Faribault County Historical Society.

Wakefield died in this house in 1910. It then passed to Edward Viehbahn, who resided in the house until 1946. The house was purchased for use as a museum, added to the National Register of Historic Places in 1980, and restored to the era of the late-nineteenth century.

The 1868 portion of the original house had a side entry hall and six other rooms. A rear wing was added in 1872 to create a kitchen and maid's quarters. Visitors enter the front hall near the side staircase. The staircase, railings, and newel post are walnut. The parlor displays an organ, a spinet piano, and a walnut desk. The adjoining dining room features a Renaissance Revival–style table and chairs set. The small room next to the dining room, furnished as an office, contains a large desk with pigeonhole compartments. The desk was found in Mr.

Wakefield's downtown law office, and it may have belonged to him.

The second story contains the family bedrooms
and the maid's quarters, the latter furnished with a set
of 1950s waterfall-style furniture. A back staircase leads
to the remodeled kitchen, which displays a 1930s wood
burning stove with other early kitchen utensils and artifacts.

The Wakefield House is now part of the Faribault
County Museum complex, which also includes the
1904 Etta C. Ross Memorial Library Museum across the
street. In addition, the Faribault County Historical Society maintains the nearby 1871 Episcopal Church of the
Good Shepherd and the History Lane complex on the
Faribault County Fairgrounds.

FILLMORE COUNTY

166. ED'S MUSEUM AND LIVING QUARTERS
100 Gold Street South, Wykoff, on Highway 5.
507-352-4205

This was the home of Edwin Julius Krueger, who lived in
the upstairs apartment and operated the Jack Sprat Food
Store below for more than fifty years. The avid collector
and hoarder died in 1989, and his will stipulated that
his building be given to the city to be operated as a museum. Today the Wykoff Historical Society operates the
museum. Special interest items include a player piano
and a collection of *Life* magazines dating back to 1938.

The two-and-one-half-story white wood-frame retail
structure was built in 1876. It features a front façade
gable and symmetrical pairs of windows. The "Jack Sprat
Food Store" sign still marks the front façade. Today the
store contains original, unopened grocery items, advertising relics, and player piano rolls.

The museum also allows tours of Ed's second-story
living quarters. One room contains toys owned by Ed

Ed's Museum and Living Quarters, Wykoff

and Lydia's son, and the rest of the apartment is filled with Ed's collections as he lived with them after his wife died. The basement contains Ed's collections of magazines and junk mail.

The Wykoff Area Historical Society also operates the Jailhouse Bed and Breakfast in the original Wykoff Jail.

167. HISTORIC FORESTVILLE 🏛 🖾

Highway 118, Forestville Township, in Forestville–Mystery Cave State Park. 507-765-2785

The village of Forestville grew up on intersecting stagecoach routes, and by 1854 this townsite along the Root River already had a small sawmill, a gristmill, and a school. At its peak in the 1860s, some 120 people lived here. Then, in 1868, the railroad shunned the steep grades of southern Fillmore county and bypassed Forestville, laying tracks ten miles north through Spring Valley. People began to move away from Forestville, and by the 1870s, its population had decreased to sixty.

Felix Meighen and Robert Foster started the village's general store in a log cabin. The Meighen Store and attached residence were built in 1856–57 out of bricks from the Forestville brickyard. In 1888 a wooden section was added to the home. The store also served as the post office and the community's bank, and residents were able to buy supplies with store credit.

The Meighens transformed their property into a working estate and ran Forestville as a company town. Citizens worked the land in exchange for housing and store credit to buy supplies. In 1905 the Meighen family moved to Preston and rented out the residence and farm, and in 1910 the store was sealed shut with all its contents intact. It remained unopened until 1960. Felix's grandchildren sold the land to the state, and the Forestville Townsite (Meighen Store) was added to the National Register of Historic Places in 1973. The site is now operated as a living-history museum by the Minnesota Historical Society, which portrays the village as it existed in 1899. Costumed interpreters portray Meighen family members, as well as the hired help. Visitors observe and interact with Forestville residents as they go about their daily lives and chores.

The brick general store filled with early-twentieth-century goods is attached to the Meighen house. The wood-frame portion of the house is painted yellow with red trim. Inside the house, visitors tour the informal family parlor, son Thomas's office, and the large working kitchen. Outside, the property is home to chickens

Historic Forestville, Forestville Township

that are historic breeds true to the 1899 setting. Behind the house a large kitchen garden contains heirloom vegetables that were grown around the turn of the century. Other original buildings on the Meighen property include an 1860s granary, 1880s wagon barn, and yellow 1894 livestock barn. The Forestville Visitor Center is located in a large gray barn, a re-creation of the original 1860s structure.

Forestville hosts a Fourth of July celebration, "Evenings of Leisure" events in the summer, and a harvest celebration in the fall. Other Forestville historic sites include the 1857 school, Foster Farmstead, sawmill, gristmill, Zumbro Hill cemetery, and distillery.

168. WASHBURN-ZITTLEMAN HOUSE MUSEUM
220 West Cortland Street, Spring Valley, west of Highway 16.
507-346-7659

The Spring Valley Community Historical Society operates the Washburn-Zittleman House Museum. In 1866 Charlie Washburn built the first three-room portion of the Victorian house, which has had later additions. The exterior has been covered with siding, but still retains its original gingerbread detail on the front gable. The great-granddaughter of the builder gave the house to the Spring Valley Community Historical Society in 1997.

Through an enclosed front porch, visitors reach an entryway that features a sizeable oak hall tree with a large beveled mirror surrounded by decorative woodwork. The sitting room has a seven-piece set of Renaissance Revival–style furniture used in the house in the 1870s, an 1883 Kimball pump organ, a beech and walnut secretary with decorative inlay details, and an Edison phonograph on a tilt-top parlor table. The dining room displays furnishings from the 1890s, including a wooden high chair that can be converted into a stroller and a set of Spode china from England. The kitchen features an 1875 cast-iron cook stove and a display of early kitchen utensils.

The second story has exhibits in former bedrooms. One displays early clothing, another features a hand-carved walnut bed and dresser set, the Halbkat room has a locally-made 1870s Eastlake bedroom set, and the children's room displays old toys and games.

The historical society's main museum is located in the former Methodist Episcopal Church, the church attended by the family of Laura Ingalls Wilder when they lived in the area in 1890–91. (The 1876 Victorian Gothic style brick and stone church is an official Laura Ingalls Wilder site and was added to the National Register of Historic Places in 1975.)

The historical society hosts an ice cream social and several Christmas teas at the house.

FREEBORN COUNTY

169. FREEBORN COUNTY HISTORICAL VILLAGE
1031 Bridge Street, Albert Lea. 507-373-8003

The Freeborn County Museum maintains a historical village with fourteen buildings, including a blacksmith shop, telephone office, post office, shoe repair shop, woodworking shop, hardware store, mill house, fully stocked general store, outhouse, one-room Big Oak School, and the 1878 North Round Prairie Church (which is still used today). The exhibit building houses farm equipment, fire-fighting equipment, antique farm implements, and five exhibits: a jail, barbershop, photographer's studio, bank, and train depot.

Three historic log cabins have been moved to the grounds. One cabin, with dovetailed corners, displays items from a post office located in Clarks Grove. Another original log cabin is furnished as a turn-of-the-century parsonage. The third log cabin was likely the first log cabin home built in Freeborn County, dating to 1853. Ole and Astri Livedalen erected it in Shell Rock Township. The one-room cabin contains typical pioneer furnishings.

GOODHUE COUNTY

170. COLLINS-GLAM HOUSE
314 Main Street North, Pine Island. 507-356-4168

Sumner Prescott Collins and Martha Ann Cron Collins built this Arts and Crafts–style house as a retirement home around 1913 on the site of an early Pine Island store run by Sumner's father. Today the Collins-Glamm House is managed by the Pine Island Area Historical Society.

The house has enclosed porches on the first and second stories. The rooms on the main floor include a kitchen, a large pantry, a dining room with a built-in buffet, a living room with a fireplace, and the front entryway. On the second floor are three bedrooms with large closets, a bathroom with original fixtures, and a sun porch. Throughout the house the flooring is the original hardwood. The house's collections include Olson Studio photos, area church histories, Pine Island High School yearbooks, military records, histories of local businesses, a biographical index of Pine Island newspapers, scrapbooks, and plat books.

171. GUNDERSON HOUSE Ⓝ
101 Gunderson Boulevard, Kenyon. 507-789-5936

The house was built in 1895 for Martin T. Gunderson, who operated a milling business and brought electric lighting to Kenyon by starting the town's first electrical company in 1896. He also operated a flour mill and cement companies. Family history tells that Mrs. Gunderson found a picture of a home she liked from the George Barber Company of Knoxville, Tennessee, a seller of "kit" homes. The precut materials came to Kenyon from Tennessee by train, and the Gundersons hired a local builder, Philip Kramer, to assemble it. Gunderson heirs gave the house and its contents to the city.

Gunderson House, Kenyon

Today the Kenyon Area Historical Society manages the house, which is owned by the city of Kenyon. The house was added to the National Register of Historic Places in 1975 and opened to the public in 1976.

The three-story Queen Anne home features front and side gables with a central hipped roof. The ends of the front gable feature a decorative "G" carved in the woodwork. An onion-shaped dome tops a second-story turret. Beneath the turret is the parlor picture window topped with a stained glass transom window.

The front entrance to the house is reached from a large open porch, which wraps around the west side of the house. On one side of the foyer is the formal parlor, which contains all family furnishings except for a Melodium and a five-piece parlor set that were donations. The family parlor, or living room, displays a late-nineteenth-century Edison phonograph and a 1920s RCA radio. In the dining room is a 1916 chandelier over the table and chairs set. An oak china cabinet and buffet are stocked with a set of Haviland Limoges china.

The second floor of the house has a sewing room, four bedrooms, and a bathroom. The master bedroom has an 1890s furniture set and a fainting couch. One of the bedrooms displays local historical artifacts including an original flour sack from the Gunderson Flour Mill. A rear staircase leads back down to the kitchen. Unique features in the kitchen include multiple flour bins and sugar bins, perhaps expected in the home of a flour-mill owner.

The historical society sponsors an annual Christmas event.

172. LARSON LOG CABIN

Main Street and East Fifth Street SW, Wanamingo.
507-824-2556

Lars E. Larson and his son Edward built this cabin in the 1850s in Section 22 of Wanamingo Township. The one-and-one-half-story cabin was moved to this site and restored in 1974. It has a centrally located front door, flanked by two windows. A local craftsman made the large table and chairs set used in the cabin. Other items of interest include the fireplace, quilts, antique clothing, and other household artifacts. An annual Fourth of July open house and other special events are held here.

HOUSTON COUNTY

173. HOUSTON COUNTY HISTORICAL SOCIETY MUSEUM

104 History Lane, Caledonia. 507-725-3884
or 507-896-2291

The Houston County Historical Society Museum on the Houston County Fairgrounds has a modern museum as well as early pioneer buildings that have been moved to the grounds. The History Lane complex includes a church, schoolhouse, store, and log cabin.

The Flatten-Swenson House was built by Targe (Olson) Flatten in 1880. He and his wife Liv Nielson Flatten raised six children, three of them born in this cabin. In 1911 Swan A. Larson purchased the home, and his descendents, the Swensons, lived in the home until the 1920s. In 1973 Warren and Wayne Swenson, both born in the cabin, donated the structure to the society.

The cabin has a large main room for the cooking and eating areas, two small bedrooms, and a second-story sleeping loft. The cabin is furnished with a hand-made Norwegian table, desk, and bed, and a cupboard built by a German pioneer.

The museum hosts a traditional Christmas, demonstrations of pioneer tasks during the Houston County Fair, and other events.

Houston County Historical Museum, Caledonia

LE SUEUR COUNTY

174. W. W. MAYO HOUSE 🏠 ℝ
118 North Main Street, Le Sueur. 507-665-3250 or 507-665-6965

This small, white, clapboard house with a cedar shake roof was the home of William Worrall Mayo and his family. When built in 1859, it was one of the few houses located in the village of Le Sueur. Today the house is situated in Louise Park in downtown Le Sueur.

W. W. Mayo immigrated to the United States from England in 1845 after studying medicine. In 1851 he married Louise Abigail Wright in Indiana, and in 1859 the Mayos moved to Le Sueur, where William built this house with the help of his brother James. In 1863 W. W. Mayo moved to Rochester, where he examined soldiers for readiness to serve in the Civil War. A year later the Mayo family relocated in Rochester, and in 1889 Dr. Mayo, along with the Sisters of St. Francis, built and established St. Mary's Hospital. W. W. Mayo's sons, Dr. Charles H. and Dr. William J., worked with their father and later founded the Mayo Clinic in Rochester.

In the early 1870s Charlotte Wright Bradley bought the Mayo property in Le Sueur and gave the house to her daughter Elizabeth on her marriage to Carson Nesbit Cosgrove in 1874. Carson became head of the Minnesota Valley Canning Company, which became the Green Giant Company in 1950.

During the 1920s residents of Le Sueur contacted the Mayo family about preserving the house. In 1935

W. W. Mayo House, Le Sueur (MHS)

Dr. Will, Dr. Charlie, and sister Gertrude presented the house to the city, which first used the building as a public library. In 1969 the house was added to the National Register of Historic Places. In 1974 the Minnesota Historical Society acquired and restored the house, which is now a museum operated by the Mayo House Interpretive Society.

Dr. Mayo's interest in Gothic architecture is evident in the home's second-story windows, which feature arched muntins. Carved brackets beneath the roofline and the slightest flare at the end of the eaves add subtle decoration. This cross-gabled house has a front gable façade, which juts out from the two side wings. The wooden front door contains four carved, inset panels echoing the Gothic arch in the window above.

The front door opens onto a small foyer with a door to the upstairs. To the right side of the foyer is a door leading to the family parlor. The large Gothic-style secretary here was built by Dr. Mayo. A door leads to the kitchen from the family parlor. Open wall shelves are stocked with dishes. The formal parlor is located to the left of the entrance foyer. Here is Louise Mayo's folding chair, a settee, a curio shelf, a drop-leaf table, and a "piecrust" table. In the second story of the house is a large former storage room, two furnished bedrooms, and a small front room where Dr. Mayo consulted with patients.

The society holds "A Giant Story" event in early August in conjunction with Le Sueur's Giant Celebration. It also hosts Fall-in-the-Valley events and Christmas tours.

MOWER COUNTY

175. GEORGE A. HORMEL HOME [NR]
208 Fourth Ave NW, Austin. 507-433-4243

John Cook, an Austin businessman, mayor, and state senator, built this home in 1871. In 1901 George A. and

Lilian Belle Hormel, the founders of Hormel Foods Corporation, bought and lived in the home. The family later gave this house to the YWCA, and in 1982 it was added to the National Register of Historic Places as the Cook-Hormel House.

The house was originally built of brick in the Italianate style. The Hormels remodeled the front by adding a neo-Classical Revival portico with four wooden Ionic columns imported from Italy and covering the exterior brick with stucco. The side wing of the house still shows the Italianate features including the bay windows and dentil wood trim and brackets underneath the roofline.

George A. Hormel Home, Austin

Inside the home, there are three fireplaces, six bedrooms, and twelve other rooms. The wood floors and additional woodwork were added by the Hormels who imported items from Europe. Quezal and Tiffany artglass are used in light fixtures throughout the home, and many windows contain beveled and stained glass. The main floor rooms include the front hall, library, office, formal living room with Italian marble fireplace and baby grand piano, dining room with the Hormels' original oak dining table and honeycomb-patterned fretwork in the ceiling, and a small breakfast room and butler's pantry. The atrium, completed in 1997, has doors leading to a Peace Garden.

The original carriage house was enlarged in 1939 to create more room for the activities of YWCA women and the Girl Scouts. The second floor bedrooms of the home are available for viewing on a tour when not being rented for short-term stays. They include an original guestroom, two servant's rooms, the family bedrooms, and a sitting room.

A Christmas open house in November features decorations provided by area merchants, and the YWCA and Girl Scouts use the building for events.

176. MOWER COUNTY HISTORICAL CENTER

1303 Sixth Avenue SW, Austin, on Mower County Fairgrounds. 507-437-6082

The Mower County Historical Center grounds have fourteen distinct buildings, as well as a steam locomotive, a suburban coach, a 1929 baggage coach, and a 1910 caboose used by the Milwaukee, Chicago, and St. Paul Railway. The historic buildings include original Mower County structures moved to this site: the 1870 rural school museum, the 1867 Christ Episcopal Church, the 1886 train depot, and the 1868 Six Mile Grove Church. A building used by George A. Hormel's company was built in the 1890s. A brick Grand Army of the Republic Hall was used by Civil War veterans for meetings. The log cabin replica on the museum grounds was built in 2000. The Rahilly Museum, the Rural Life Museum, and the Pioneer Museum all house Mower County, pastoral, and pioneer history exhibits. Other modern structures include a fireman's museum, a blacksmith shop, a communications museum, and the H. J. Williams collection of Native American artifacts.

NICOLLET COUNTY

177. EUGENE ST. JULIEN COX HOUSE Ⓝ

500 Washington Avenue North, St. Peter.
507-934-2160 or 507-934-4309

The 1871 Cox House is a unique Gothic Italianate wood-frame house. The fully restored home is furnished in the late Victorian style with a blend of original and donated pieces. The Cox family owned the house until 1969 when it was given to the Nicollet County Historical Society, and the society operates the house today. The first level of restoration work was completed in 1971 and the house was opened as a museum. The house was added to the National Register of Historic Places in 1970.

Eugene St. Julien Cox and his wife Mariah came to St. Peter in 1857, where he established a private law practice. Cox served in the military in the Civil War, and in 1862 he was chosen to lead St. Peter–area volunteers to the defense of New Ulm during the US-Dakota War. Cox was elected the town's first mayor, served as a state legislator, and in 1878 became a district judge.

The house has a blend of the Italianate and Gothic styles, perhaps selected by Cox from plan books. The square, paneled columns on the front porch are in the Italianate style. Bay windows, typical rectangle windows, and rounded-topped windows were all used in the house. The "witch's hat"–shaped roof of the tower and the carved decorative trim under the eaves with arcs and other fretwork designs are Gothic features.

Visitors enter the home from the front corner porch. Tours begin in the formal parlor, which features a restored Eastlake table found in the home. Cox's daughter, shown in the 1913 photograph on the table, was the first female mayor of St. Peter. A door leads to the family parlor, where a suite of Empire Revival–style furniture with carved serpent heads is displayed. The rear corner study's bookcase and desk are original to the house. In the dining room, the table is set with china, glassware, and serving pieces. The restored kitchen features a dry sink and pump, a table set with tea-leaf–patterned stoneware, and a clock from the Nicollet County Courthouse. The front foyer has a carved, cantilevered staircase handcrafted in St. Paul.

Eugene St. Julien Cox House, St. Peter

All the bedrooms originally had closets, which were taxed as rooms at the time. Visitors tour the blue, pink, and yellow bedrooms, and the hall ends at the master bedroom, which has recreated wallpaper and an Eastlake bedroom set with a marble-topped vanity. The restored carriage house displays a 1917 Sears & Roebuck buggy, a hand-crafted cutter sled, a 1908 Studebaker Surry, and an 1888 child's sleigh.

The society hosts a Victorian Christmas, garden parties, and old-fashioned perennial plant sales in the summer. The Nicollet County Historical Society is head-quartered at the Treaty History Site north of St. Peter. The society also operates three state historic sites: Traverse des Sioux, Harkin Store, and Fort Ridgely.

OLMSTED COUNTY

178. HERITAGE HOUSE
225 First Avenue NW, Rochester, at Third Street NW.
507-286-9208 or 507-288-4692

The 1856 Heritage House is located in Rochester's downtown Central Park. The house originally belonged to Timothy and Eliza Whiting and was located about a block from its current location. When the vacant house fell into great disrepair and was scheduled for demolition, the non-profit Heritage Associates, Inc., formed in order to save it. In 1971 the house was moved on a flat bed to its current location, and in 1973 it was opened for tours.

The Italianate-style house features a hipped roof and an open front porch. The entrance to the house is on the left side, with a pair of narrow two-paned windows on the right side. The porch's carved brackets are typical of the Italianate style. The south side of the house has unique faux windows with shutters.

The front parlor has a Hazelton Brothers square grand piano. The second parlor has an Eastlake-style fainting couch, a crazy quilt, three needlepoint-covered Eastlake chairs, and an Eastlake pump organ. There

Heritage House, Rochester

are double glass doors, built-in bookcases, and molding salvaged from the Kahler house used in this room. The dining room has original Whiting family Renaissance Revival–style walnut chairs around the table. The kitchen has an original cabinet, a cast-iron woodstove, an early phone, and a zinc-lined sink.

On the second floor a small hallway leads to three rooms. One room is a children's room, the master bedroom has an Eastlake walnut suite, and a third room has a three-piece set of "cottage furniture" with painted faux graining.

179. MAYOWOOD MANSION [NR]
3720 Mayowood Road SW, Rochester, near Highway 52.
507-282-9447

Mayowood was the home of Dr. Charles Horace Mayo, co-founder with his brother, Dr. William James Mayo, of the world-renowned Mayo Clinic in Rochester. "Dr. Charlie" married Edith Graham, who was Rochester's first trained nurse.

The couple's thirty-eight room home of poured concrete was originally sited on 3,000 acres. The estate included eight farms and elaborate gardens. The mansion, built in 1910–11, is based on designs specified by Charles and Edith. The Mayos enlarged the house several times, and by 1936 final addition was completed. The Mayo's son, Dr. Charles W. (called "Dr. Chuck"), and his wife Alice continued to remodel the house within the 1936 footprint of the house.

The house and ten acres were donated to the Olmsted County Historical Society in 1965. In 1970 the house was added to the National Register of Historic Places. The Mayowood Historic District, added to the National Register of Historic Places in 1982, includes the mansion, Ivy Lodge, and the farm and greenhouse complexes, built from 1908 through the 1920s.

The large mansion is a blend of styles. The concrete façade and roof with the sweeping front stairs and terraces offer the feel of an Italian villa, but the unified horizontal bands of windows, hipped roofs, and fifth-story lookout tower are in the Prairie School style.

Tours start at the side entrance and lead upstairs to an open foyer. A narrow hall leads from the foyer to a 1960s kitchen. A door from the kitchen leads to a library, which features paneling created out of reclaimed doors from a Rochester school. The French doors of the study (for former porch) contain stained glass designs from the Linden Art Glass Company in Chicago. Double-paneled doors lead to the music room, which contains a pipe organ with a built-in oak cabinet that hides the pipes.

Visitors then step down through the gilt doorway into a 25-by-46-foot living room. The English Tudor influence is felt here with the oak-beamed ceiling, oak-paneled walls, and stone fireplace. Double doors lead to the dining room with a children's table on one side and a main dining room table on the other. Visitors then tour the butler's pantry, kitchen, servants' dining room, and a gallery that was used as a breakfast area. The gallery leads to the main foyer hall with an elevator and stairs that lead to the second floor.

Upstairs are Chuck and Alice's master bedroom, his and her marble bathrooms, and a guestroom with a hand-carved walnut four-poster bed. The house has eleven bedrooms and eight complete baths.

Mayowood hosts annual garden tours and decorated Christmas tours. The site is operated by the Olmsted County Historical Society.

180. WILLIAM DEE LOG CABIN AND GEORGE STOPPEL FARMSTEAD

1195 West Circle Drive SW, Rochester, west of Highway 52. 507-282-9447

The grounds of the History Center of Olmsted County contain two historic structures moved to the site, and a historic farmstead sits on land adjacent to the museum.

Moved to the site are the 1862 William Dee Log Cabin and the 1885 Hadley Valley Schoolhouse.

The one-room Dee cabin features whitewashed logs and a cedar shake roof. William and Bridget Dee built it in the spring of 1862 in what is now the city of Rochester. In 1972 the cabin was moved to the current location.

The George Stoppel Farmstead and grounds are part of the museum, but the buildings are not open to the public. The Stoppel family first lived in a root cave on the property in 1856. The 1861 limestone house, barn, and two-story shed and smokehouse were added to the National Register of Historic Places in 1975.

The History Center's main museum is located in a modern building filled with interpretive exhibits detailing the history of Rochester and the surrounding area. Their research library and archives contain maps, photographs, diaries, journals, and books relating to the history of Olmsted County and southeastern Minnesota. The active group sponsors many events throughout the year including the Yaggy Colby History Lecture Series, a cemetery walk, the Roosters Classic Vintage Baseball Festival, and a hands-on history event.

181. PLUMMER HOUSE OF THE ARTS [NR]

1091 Plummer Lane, Rochester, near Highway 52.
507-281-6160

The Plummer House of the Arts is located in the English Tudor mansion built between 1917 and 1924 for Dr. Henry Stanley Plummer and his wife Daisy. Dr. Plummer collaborated with architect Thomas Farr Ellerbe to create this landmark home. The house was added to the National Register of Historic Places in 1975. Originally the Plummer House was located on a sixty-five-acre estate, but today the property has been trimmed to eleven acres and is now operated by the Rochester Park and Recreation Department.

Dr. Plummer worked at the Mayo Clinic from 1901

until 1936. He is credited with establishing the record keeping system, helping design clinic buildings including the landmark Plummer Building (1926–28), and inventing the pneumatic tube, used for clinic communications. His wife, Daisy Berkman Plummer, was a concert pianist and patron of the arts.

The Tudor home's exterior is crafted from stucco with cut stone, brick, and cross-timber detailing. Casement windows and a slate roof add to the Tudor elements. Inside, the hallway features oak-beamed ceilings, floors made with inlaid tile, and travertine marble imported from Italy on the walls. On the far end of the foyer is Dr. Plummer's study, complete with an intercom control center and built-in bookshelves. Dr. Plummer's desk is original to the home, as is all other furniture on display in the house.

The foyer opens directly onto a 20-by-40-foot living room with oak paneling, plaster ceilings featuring the carved Tudor rose emblem, two crystal chandeliers, and a fireplace. The dining room is reached from the foyer and has a Baroque dining table and chairs. Both rooms contain French doors leading to separate sunrooms. The original pantry, kitchen, laundry room, and service bathroom

Plummer House of the Arts, Rochester

are located in a wing that connects to the garage. The second floor contains the bedrooms for the family and the hired help. The rooms have been redecorated with new wallpapers and fabrics, but the furniture is original to the family. One guestroom, called the Ellerbe room, displays original architectural drawings of the home.

In the hallway are stairs leading to the third floor ballroom. This large room now is outfitted with mirrors and ballet barres on the walls reflecting the home's use as an arts center in the 1970s. At the far end of the room is a massive fireplace with flanking alcoves where built-in benches and windows created smoking nooks.

Outside, visitors find elaborate formal gardens, as well as the mansion's signature stone water tower.

182. RICHARD W. SEARS HOUSE
305 Main Street North, Stewartville. 507-533-6470

The Richard W. Sears House is the birthplace of the founder of Sears, Roebuck, & Company. Nicholas Gaskigar built the wood-frame, one-and-one-half-story house in 1860. Charles Stewart, for whom Stewartville was named, also lived in the house for a time. James and Eliza Burton Sears gave birth to son Richard W. Sears in this house in 1863. Today the house is maintained by the Stewartville Area Historical Society, which purchased it from the estate of John Lins.

James Sears was an early Stewartville pioneer who worked as a blacksmith, and the family lived in the house until 1869 when they relocated to nearby Spring Valley. Son Richard first worked as a station agent for the railroad. He had the opportunity to purchase a shipment of watches and resold them at a profit. This inspired him to start a mail order business, which he operated for a time in Minneapolis and then later Chicago. After he hired watch repairman Alvah Roebuck, the two joined together as Sears, Roebuck, & Company in 1893.

The home's main entrance is located off the front porch, which, along with the side wing, was added in the early-twentieth century. Additional remodeling was done in the 1930s. The rear kitchen, renovated in 2002, features a 1920s dry sink, a gas stove, a refrigerator, and period cooking utensils. The adjacent dining room has items that were sold in the Sears catalog, including a set of tea-leaf ironstone dishes, Conley cameras, and a Silvertone radio. The home's living room features furniture that was originally used in the Stewartville Opera House and a collection of Sears catalogs. The home's three bedrooms on the second floor have artifacts from Stewartville residents.

The museum holds a Christmas open house, as well as an annual Cabin Fever Flea Market fundraiser, held at the Civic Center.

RICE COUNTY

183. ALEXANDER FARIBAULT HOUSE

*12 First Avenue NE, Faribault. 507-224-7913
or 507-332-2121*

The Alexander Faribault House is a white, two-story Greek Revival–style wood-frame house built in 1853 above the banks of the Straight River in Faribault's namesake city. This was the first house built in the Cannon River Valley, and it once served as a community center, chapel, polling place, and meeting hall. The house is now owned by the Rice County Historical Society, which bought the house in 1945 and gradually restored it.

Alexander was the son of fur trader Jean Baptiste Faribault, who built his family's house in Mendota across the river from Fort Snelling and near the property of Henry Sibley, Minnesota's first elected governor. Alexander Faribault was at one time Henry Sibley's secretary. In 1825 Alexander Faribault married Elizabeth Graham, and in 1826 they established a trading post for the American Fur Company on Cannon Lake. After several moves he established the post in 1844 on land that became the city of Faribault.

The Faribault family lived in this house for three years. The sizeable house was built at a substantial cost of $4,000 in 1853. The front entrance to the house is located off a simple porch. The chimneys are located in the front and rear gable ends of the house.

The house originally had nine rooms, including a music room, parlor, sitting room, office, kitchen, summer kitchen, sewing room, and second-story bedrooms. The front foyer features a hall tree that was original to the house and the staircase to the second floor. Doors lead to the parlor, dining room, and office. The parlor walls have murals

Alexander Faribault House, Faribault

painted under the windows by Alexander's father, Jean Baptiste. On display is a Faribault family music stand, an 1881 Steinway and Sons piano, and the family Bible. A doorway leads from the parlor to the dining room, which has a Rococo Revival–style table and chairs. The office, adjacent to the dining room, contains a large Wooton's Rotary Desk.

The staircase off the foyer leads to the second floor. In the large open hallway of the second floor hangs a large mirror made in Connecticut after the Revolutionary War. The hallway has one of the two closets in the house; inside one is a unique chamber-pot set decorated with a paisley design. Three other bedrooms display period furnishings and artifacts. Highlights include a spindle rope bed with a cornhusk mattress, a cannonball rope bed with a crocheted coverlet, a fainting couch, a display of early hats, a dresser with a carved fig leaf pattern, and a reed rocker made at a furniture factory in Faribault.

A door from the hall leads to a more recent building addition now used for displays of local historical artifacts. Items of interest include an 1867 cast iron stove and an 1869 Swedish trunk filled with early clothes. There is a wooden box with a sitz bath from the Faribault hospital, a wicker baby buggy and cradle, a leather sofa, a baking table with cast iron tools, a crazy quilt, a handmade large spinning wheel, and three Singer sewing machines. Interesting children's and doll furniture are also on display.

184. RICE COUNTY HISTORICAL SOCIETY
1814 Second Avenue NW (County Road 3), Faribault, north of Hwy 60. 507-332-2121

Founded in 1926, the Rice County Historical Society is located on the Rice County Fairgrounds. The society's grounds have an 1850s log cabin, the 1884 one-room Pleasant Valley School, and the 1860s Holy Innocents Episcopal Church from Cannon City.

Sever Holgrimson Vold built the log cabin in Wheeling Township north of Faribault. The cabin was most likely built in 1857–58; for a time after 1897, it was used as a school. The Rudningen family owned the property and rented the cabin from 1902 until 1953. In the early 1960s, the cabin was donated and moved to this site. The cabin is furnished with a rug loom, an early table and chairs set, and a rope bed.

A modern museum building housing exhibits and archives is located on the Rice County Fairgrounds. The research center is available for genealogical and local history research.

SIBLEY COUNTY

185. AUGUST F. POEHLER HOUSE
700 Main Street, Henderson, on County Road 19.
507-248-3818

The Sibley County Historical Society Museum is located in the 1884 August F. Poehler House. Poehler was a German immigrant and early settler of Henderson. His son, Minneapolis resident August L. Poehler, was the Sibley County Historical Society's first president and a former Henderson merchant. The house was sold in 1948 to the society for use as a museum, and the house was added to the National Register of Historic Places in 1982.

The modified Eastlake Gothic brick house has a slate roof. Designed by George Pass, the house is a blend of Gothic elements mixed with the Queen Anne style and influenced by Italianate designs. The central hipped roof has two cross gables, one front and one side, with a corner gable between. The second-story windows and seven

August F. Poehler House, Henderson

chimneys feature brick trim and detailing. The keystone lintels placed in the segmented arches above the rectangular windows show the influence of the Italianate style. Brick quoins form the wall edges, and a stone belt course marks the line between the two floors.

The Poehler House had the latest technologies of its time, including an upstairs bathroom and central heating. Radiators and registers from the combination steam-and-wood central heating system remain in the house. Only minor changes have been made in the interior rooms, which display the collection of the historical society.

An 1858 log cabin built by Christian Didra, a German immigrant to Henderson, was purchased and moved to the museum grounds in 1969.

STEELE COUNTY

186. VILLAGE OF YESTERYEAR
1448 Austin Road, Steele County Fairgrounds, Owatonna. 507-451-1420

The Steele County Historical Society operates the Village of Yesteryear. In 1962 the society acquired the 1891 St. Wenceslaus of Moravia Church from Saco, and the Steele County Fair Board offered the land on which the village is now located.

Tours start at the center of the village at the Dunnell House. This mansion was built in 1868–69 for the family of Mark Hill Dunnell, a Maine native elected to the Minnesota legislature in 1867. Dunnell also served in the US House of Representatives for fourteen years beginning in 1870. His house was later a part of the Pillsbury Military Academy and the Pillsbury Baptist College. The house was moved to this site in 1969 and opened to the public in the early 1970s. Dunnell family descendents have provided artifacts displayed in the house.

The Italianate house has a low-pitched, hipped roof topped by a square cupola that recalls New England architectural styles. Brackets under the eaves, as well as the hooded windows, are usual features of the Italianate style.

Visitors to the home first enter the library. The highlight of the room is a cane made from cedar taken from a home of Christopher Columbus, with accompanying documents of authenticity. The dining room features a large oak table set with a rotating display of china from the early-twentieth century. A glass decanter displayed here was once used to serve President Abraham Lincoln. The kitchen features the original flooring and fireplace and a 1920s wood-burning stove. Visitors tour the family parlor, with its 1867 square grand piano and a working Edison phonograph. A fainting couch located in the bay window can be folded up to create a love seat.

On the second floor are the master bedroom, a bathroom, and a children's room. A fashion room is filled with hats, purses, clothing, jewelry, and a button collection. The Pillsbury Military Academy room and the US military collection room pay tribute to the school that used the residence.

Historic structures on the village grounds include the 1891 St. Wenceslaus of Moravia Church from Saco, the 1899 Milwaukee Railroad depot from Bixby, an 1896 blacksmith shop, the 1850s Owatonna town hall, the 1856 District 14 schoolhouse, and two log cabins. Historic schoolhouses were reused to create a general store with post office and a museum of professions. The modern farm machinery building showcases farm implements from throughout Steele County. Two log cabins were also moved to the village.

The historical society sponsors Victorian teas, Christmas events, and a Harvest Fest, and the village comes alive with costumed interpreters during the Steele County Fair.

WASECA COUNTY

187. BAILEY-LEWER HOUSE
401 Second Avenue NE, Waseca, north of Highway 14.
507-835-7700

In 1868 Dayton Smith built the home now known as the Bailey-Lewer House. An accused horse thief, Smith was about to be hanged when he was rescued and then disappeared. Smith's wife sold the house in 1872 to Philo Calvin Bailey, who owned the first hardware store in Waseca County. In 1907 the Lewer family purchased the house and kept it in the family until 1991. The Waseca County Historical Society purchased the house, which was in great disrepair, in 1992. In 1994, the restored house was added to the National Register of Historic Places. A research center opened in it in 1998.

The Bailey-Lewer House is one of Waseca's oldest remaining homes. The brick Italianate residence features

Bailey-Lewer House, Waseca

a typical hipped roof and front verandah. The window layout is symmetrical with two-over-two windows on the sides and the second story of the front façade of the house. There is a telescoped rear section, with a rear side porch off what was originally the kitchen.

The home's front door leads to a hallway with a staircase to the second level offices. On the main floor, the front parlor and adjoining dining room have restored wood floors, reproduction wallpaper, and shelves full of research material. Many pieces in the center are antiques from local government offices. The county auditor's double-sided slanted worktable fills the center of the former dining room. A table from the first county courthouse, located in Wilton from 1854 until 1870, now holds computers and microfiche readers. The rear of the house, originally the kitchen, has more workspace, a modernized kitchen, and storage space.

The Waseca County Historical Society's main museum is in the former 1917 Waseca Methodist Church across the street from the research center. The society also maintains the Hodgson Hall of agricultural artifacts and the District 41 county school located at the Waseca County Fairgrounds.

188. FARMAMERICA

7367 Three-Hundred-and-Sixtieth Avenue, Waseca, at County Roads 2 and 17. 507-835-2052

A modern barn-like visitor's center is the center of Farmamerica. This 120-acre site, also known as the Minnesota Agricultural Interpretive Center, was established by the state legislature in 1978 to tell the story of the state's agriculture. Now, 150 years of agricultural history are portrayed for visitors who stroll Time Lane Road past a cornfield to the village buildings.

An 1850s settlement farm includes a log home, a barn, a log and sod house, and a sod dugout house. A split-rail fence encloses native prairie plantings. Visitors pass a birch grove and a swamp area to reach the 1881

Brighton Methodist Church, moved here in 1987, and the Gallagher School, which is from St. Mary's Township in Waseca County. A dairy farm includes a white Upright-and-Wing-style farmhouse, a barn, and other outbuildings. This farm is original to this property. A blacksmith shop is located in another historical building. The Condon Mill building is from Waseca, and it operated as a feed mill until 1989. Live cows, a hay field, and hay wagons are on display.

Farmamerica holds special events in the summer and the fall.

Farmamerica, Waseca

WINONA COUNTY

189. ARCHES MUSEUM OF PIONEER LIFE

US Highway 14, west of Winona between Stockton and Lewiston. 507-523-2111 or 507-454-2723

The Arches Museum of Pioneer Life is an example of the early phenomenon of roadside museums that were operated by individuals on their private property. The museum is named for the original stone railroad-bridge arches located nearby. Walter Rahn, who died in 1984, created this museum to house his collections of early

Minnesota pioneer artifacts. His folk art and handmade working models are also on display.

Today a modern museum building is operated by the Winona County Historical Society. It is filled with artifacts collected or made by Rahn. The museum's grounds include a furnished 1862 log cabin, a barn with early farm implements, an 1862 one-room schoolhouse, and a covered bridge over a stream. An original well, a windmill, and early carriages and farm implements are housed in a covered shed.

The 1862 log cabin built by Jonas Johnson comes from Fremont Township in Winona County. The Hans Hill family lived in it until 1956. Bertram Boyum donated the cabin to the Winona County Historical Society, and it was moved here in 1968. The cabin contains a spinning wheel, treadle sewing machine, rocking chair, a primitive hutch, and an early cook stove. A log barn built on a farm in St. Charles Township in Winona County was moved to the museum in 1968.

190. HISTORIC BUNNELL HOUSE [NR]
Near Highway 14/61, Homer. 507-454-2723
or 507-452-7575

The Winona County Historical Society has operated the Bunnell House museum since 1954. The home of the first permanent settler in Winona County, the house was added to the National Register of Historic Places in 1973.

The Bunnell House was built in the early 1850s of unfinished board and battens cut from northern white pine. Remarkably, the house has never been painted, and the boards are now weathered. The style of the house is the Cottage Gothic Revival, presumably based on the patterns popularized by Andrew Jackson Downing during the 1840s–50s. The home is built into the hillside, with one wall formed of stone. The home features two levels of porches, with medieval crosses cut into the cornices created along the roofline. The unfinished wood and use of natural stone materials fulfilled Downing's prescriptions that a home fit in with its natural environs.

Willard Bradley Bunnell and his wife Matilda Desnoyer Bunnell first built a log cabin home here in 1849 after Wapasha, a Dakota leader living near Winona, reportedly gave his permission to build at the location. Besides founding the town, Bunnell served as its first postmaster. After he died in 1861, Matilda raised six surviving children here.

The family used all three levels of the house, including the basement, which is on the ground floor because the house is built into a hill. A kitchen, a pantry, and a small bedroom, possibly for hired help, are on the ground floor. A cast-iron stove and collections of early cooking utensils are on display in the kitchen. The second floor contains the parlor, dining room, front hall, and an office. The carpeting in the parlor is of the 1850s period. The piano is reputed to be the first one brought to Winona on a steamboat in the 1860s. The office is furnished as a post office and office for Willard Bunnell's fur trading, surveying, and other business endeavors.

On the third floor are three family bedrooms and a guestroom. These rooms display heirloom quilts and period clothing, as well as bedroom furnishings. Front porches on the second and third floors offer a view of the home's grounds. A carriage house dates from around 1900. The grounds are landscaped and highlight native plantings.

The historical society offers summer programs for children and an annual Heritage Fair.

191. MARNACH HOUSE Ⓝ

Whitewater State Park, Highway 74, Altura, north of Elba near County Road 26. 507-932-3007

A visit to the Marnach House offers a rare opportunity to view authentic Luxembourg house construction techniques. Masons Nicholas Majerus and John Marnach immigrated from Rambrouch, Luxembourg, with their families in 1857 and settled with other Luxembourg immigrants in Whitewater Township near Elba. They built this house between 1857 and 1869 in the Luxembourg *Quereinhaus* style. The house and surrounding farmland were used until 1949, when they were acquired by the State of Minnesota.

In the 1920s local citizens lobbied to establish Whitewater State Park, and the state purchased additional land to create the 28,000-acre Whitewater Wildlife Management Area adjacent to the park. Today, the Marnach House is reached via a hiking path inside the wildlife management area. In 1978 the house was added to the National Register of Historic Places as part of a plan to save the house.

The house's restoration is unusual. Work by historian Mary Nilles, a native of nearby Rollingstone and an active researcher of the house's history, led to involvement by the Grand Duchy of Luxembourg, and Luxembourg stonemasons and artisans, working with many nearby residents. The Minnesota Department of Natural Resources and the Minnesota Historical Society were involved in the restoration, which was completed in 1993.

The house has six rooms. Two-foot-thick stone walls are covered in white plaster. A curved staircase leads to the second floor from the kitchen. The restoration included replacing the roof, reinforcing the walls, reconstructing parts of the walls, installing new flooring, repairing plaster, and replacing the doors, windows, and shutters. The windows have working wooden shutters.

Special events held at the house include a fall leaf tour and winter sleigh rides. Open house tours are held one Sunday per month in the summer months.

REFERENCES

In addition to using the books listed below, I relied on published material provided by museum staff in the form of pamphlets, docent guides, newspaper articles, and other information. I took guided tours at many of the museums and telephoned or spoke in person with many tour guides and museum directors. In addition, I consulted museum websites to glean information for this text. Many thanks go to the staff and volunteers who helped me along the way.

Arthur, A. *Minnesota Museums: Monuments, Festivals, & Historic Sites*. Cambridge, Minn.: Adventure Publications, 2004.

Berman, L. *Landmarks—Old and New. Minneapolis and St. Paul and Surrounding Areas*. Minneapolis: Nodin Press, 1988.

Federal Writers' Project of the Works Progress Administration. *The WPA Guide to Minnesota*. 1938; St. Paul: Minnesota Historical Society Press, 1985.

French, E. S. *Exploring the Twin Cities with Children*. Minneapolis: Nodin Press, Inc., 1996.

Gebhard, D. and T. Martinson. *A Guide to the Architecture of Minnesota*. Minneapolis: University of Minnesota Press, 1977.

Green, S. E., and B. Hilowitz (editors). *Historic Houses of America*. New York: Simon and Schuster, 1980.

Kennedy, R. *Historic Homes of Minnesota*. St. Paul: Minnesota Historical Society Press, 2006.

Ketchum Jr., W. C. *The Antique Hunter's Guide to American Furniture: Chests, cupboards, desks, & other pieces*. New York: Black Dog & Leventhal Publishers, 2000.

McAlester, V. and L. *A Field Guide to American Houses*. New York: Alfred A. Knopf, 1992.

Morse, J. *Minnesota Free: The State's Best No-Charge Attractions*. Minneapolis: Nodin Press, 1998.

Nord, M. A. *The National Register of Historic Places in Minnesota: A Guide*. St. Paul: Minnesota Historical Society Press, 2003.

Sandeen, E. R. *St. Paul's Historic Summit Avenue*. St. Paul: Living Historical Museum, Macalester College, 1978.

Schwartz, M. D. *The Antique Hunter's Guide to American Furniture: Tables, chairs, sofas, & beds*. New York: Black Dog & Leventhal Publishers, 2000.

Svendsen, G. R. *Hennepin County History: An Illustrated Essay*. Minneapolis: Hennepin County Historical Society, 1976.

Werle, S. *An American Gothic: The Life & Times & Legacy of William Gates LeDuc*. South St. Paul: Dakota County Historical Society, 2004.

Winckler, S. *The Smithsonian Guide to Historic America: The Great Lake States*. New York: Stewart, Tabori, and Chang, 1989.

INDEX

ALSO AVAILABLE FROM THE MINNESOTA HISTORICAL SOCIETY PRESS

The Minnesota Book of Days: An Almanac of State History
by Tony Greiner

A fun and fascinating day-by-day account of Minnesota history, chronicling important events, famous firsts, notable individuals, and interesting incidents. A perfect gift for any fan of Minnesota history and trivia.

$13.95, paper, ISBN 0-87351-416-5

Minnesota History along the Highways: A Guide to Historic Markers and Sites
Compiled by Sarah P. Rubinstein

A handy travel guide to more than 254 historic markers, 60 geologic markers, and 29 state historic monuments throughout the state.

$13.95, paper, ISBN 0-87351-456-4

The National Register of Historic Places in Minnesota: A Guide
Compiled by Mary Ann Nord

A county-by-county guide to Minnesota's more than 1,500 holdings on the National Register of Historic Places, the country's official list of historic properties.

$13.95, paper, ISBN 0-87351-448-3

The Pocket Guide to Minnesota Place Names
by Michael Fedo

The pocket version of the authoritative *Minnesota Place Names*, 3rd Edition. This handy guide is the perfect companion for anyone who travels the highways and waterways of the North Star state.

$11.95, paper, ISBN 0-87351-424-6

A Guide to F. Scott Fitzgerald's St. Paul
by John J. Koblas

A handy guide to more than 100 places associated with famed author F. Scott Fitzgerald, including boyhood homes, favorite places, and homes of friends and family.

$9.95, paper, ISBN 0-87351-513-7

Six Feet Under: A Graveyard Guide to Minnesota
by Stew Thornley

Perfect for road trippers and armchair travelers alike, this handy guide locates the final resting places and tells the stories of more than 375 famous and infamous Minnesotans.

$14.95, paper, ISBN 0-87351-514-5

JOIN THE MINNESOTA HISTORICAL SOCIETY TODAY! IT'S THE BEST DEAL IN HISTORY!

The Minnesota Historical Society is the nation's premier state historical society. Founded in 1849, the Society collects, preserves, and tells the story of Minnesota's past through innovative museum exhibits, extensive collections and libraries, educational programs, historic sites, and book and magazine publishing. Membership support is vital to the Society's ability to serve its ever-broadening and increasingly diverse public with programs and services that are educational, engaging, and entertaining.

What are the benefits of membership?

Members enjoy:

- A subscription to the quarterly magazine *Minnesota History;*
- *History Matters* newsletter and events calendar;
- Regular free admission to the Society's 26 historic sites and museums;
- Discounts on purchases from the Minnesota Historical Society Press and on other purchases and services in our Museum Stores, Library, Café Minnesota, and much more;
- Select reciprocal benefits at more than 70 historical organizations and museums in over 40 states through Time Travelers; and
- Satisfaction of knowing your membership helps support the Society's programs.

Membership fees/categories:

- $65 Household (2 adults and children under 18 in same household and grandchildren under 18)
- $55 Senior Household (age 65+ for 2 adults and children under 18 in same household and grandchildren under 18)
- $55 Individual (1 adult)
- $45 Senior Individual (age 65+ for 1 adult)
- $125 Associate
- $250 Contributing
- $500 Sustaining
- $1,000 North Star Circle

Join by phone or e-mail. To order by phone, call 651-259-3131 (TTY 651-282-6073) or e-mail membership@mnhs.org. Benefits extend one year from date of joining.